Flights

- People to Places in Style -

A Pictorial History Of Flights Coaches 1923–2002

Flights
- *People to Places in Style* -
A Pictorial History Of Flights Coaches 1923–2002

Andrew Roberts

BREWIN BOOKS

Published by Brewin Books Ltd
Studley, Warwickshire B80 7LG
in 2010

www.brewinbooks.com

© Andrew Roberts 2010

All rights reserved.

ISBN: 978-1-85858-436-2

British Library Cataloguing in Publication Data
A Catalogue record for this book is available from the British Library.

Typeset in Times
Printed in Great Britain by
Information Press Ltd.

Contents

Flights Coaches Story – Part One: 1923-1973   1

Flights Coaches Story – Part Two: 1977-2002 onwards   81

Fleet list for Flights Coach Travel   157

Acknowledgements

Ken Flight, and Geoff Flight for all assistance provided in researching the company history, and for privileged access to their photographic archive.

Alan Mills, from the Omnibus Society for providing the detailed fleet history.

And to others who have kindly provided photographs from their collection, and given permission for them to be reproduced.

Part One: 1923-1973

The name Flights is well known and highly respected in the world of coach travel. Under control of the Flight family, the company was noted for its high standards of presentation, not just of its vehicles, but also customer service throughout the whole organisation.

The company can trace its roots back to 1913 when Frank Flight acquired a Daimler taxi. After leaving school, Frank served as an apprentice with the Wolseley Motor Company and, later Daimler. His training and qualifications would have given him employment within the motor trade almost anywhere, however Frank decided that he would be his own boss and acquired a garage at 83 Victoria Road in the Aston district of Birmingham. The business progressed well, with a second taxi being acquired, however the start of the Great War caused a temporary halt in further development.

A Sergeant in the Territorial Army, Frank Flight was posted to Belgium. He later served in France and in 1916 was wounded and repatriated to a military hospital in Colchester. During his convalescence he planned to buy an Army ambulance at the end of the war and convert it to dual-purpose use.

Following the end of the war, Frank bought his ex-Army ambulance and converted it, as planned. During the week it had a flat bed, drop sided, body fitted and was used to make deliveries of parcels, furniture and other goods. At weekends a charabanc body was fitted and pleasure trips were operated.

The passenger carrying part of the business was developed with additional taxis being acquired, and eventually the delivery service was discontinued and another coach purchased. As the business grew, a move to a larger garage at 114 Victoria Road was made.

Two Daimler charabancs were acquired in the early 1920's and a bus service was operated serving Witton, Perry Barr and Kingstanding – the route was run in competition with Birmingham City Transport. During the great strike in 1926 Flights maintained their operations – Frank Flight running the gauntlet of striking bus crews. Private bus services were however banned in the City of Birmingham in 1928 so Flights concentrated on coach hire, pleasure trips and their taxi service.

By 1939 a fleet of five coaches and several taxis were operated alongside the garage business. By this time Frank Flight's wife, Amy, helped him in the business dealing with all of the office work.

The outbreak of the Second World War again caused a temporary halt in operations. Taxis were converted into ambulances or to tow fire-fighting equipment, and the Army commandeered coaches from the fleet for Military use. One coach was used to distribute gas masks to civilians, who entered at the front of the vehicle and left by the rear emergency exit following fitting and brief lessons of the use of their protective mask.

Any drivers that had not been called up for service were re-trained as auxiliary fire fighters. Mrs Flight became a fire service administrator, and Frank Flight a commander in the Special Police – the unpaid, part-time, Police force. It is said that he frequently picked up smaller incendiary bombs and carried them in the boot of his car to a bomb disposal unit! During 1940 the family home and the garage were damaged in an air raid – fortunately the family had taken refuge in their Anderson shelter and escaped any injuries.

Two of the commandeered coaches were returned in 1943 and were employed to take workers to the Spitfire factory at Castle Bromwich from their safe homes in Tamworth.

Following the suspension of hostilities, and despite continued petrol rationing, the business began to grow once more. The post-war coach fleet consisted of a Maudslay and a Bedford WTB. These were joined in 1946 by a Burlingham bodied Maudslay SF40 which had been new in 1935 to Don Everall of Wolverhampton. Fitted with a "long stroke" engine ahead of the front axle, Ken Flight recalls that it was excellent when travelling on flat roads but was hopelessly underpowered at any incline. In an attempt to rectify this problem an engine from a GMC tank was installed but unfortunately this was not too successful – whilst it was now good on hills it would only manage low maximum speeds.

The first new coach for nearly 10 years arrived in 1948 – a Maudslay Marathon 3 with 33-seat Santus body. Two further coaches were acquired in 1949 and others throughout the 1950's. The 1960's and 70's saw regular purchases of new vehicles.

Frank's son, Ken, joined the family business following his demobilisation from the RAF. Unfortunately Frank Flight died in 1951, but Ken took over from his father and set his sights on building a first-class coach operation with the finest coaches and the best drivers.

With a post-war public eager for pleasure trips and holiday travel, Ken obtained licences to run summer coastal services and excursions under the

Flights – People to Places in Style

Frank Flight's first garage at 83. Victoria Road, Aston. A Daimler taxi is in view – Frank Flight is standing to the right of the picture. *Ken Flight collection*

Two early taxis operated by Frank Flight – note the "FF" registration. *Ken Flight collection*

The business later moved to a larger garage at 114 Victoria Road. In this view Frank Flight is pictured with garage and driving staff and daughter Marjorie. *Ken Flight collection*

"Flights Tours" title. A new Burlingham Seagull bodied AEC Regal was purchased in 1953 and was followed by another four similar vehicles, which gave Flight's a modern fleet of under floor engine coaches when much of the competition still ran half-cab designs.

Aston Villa Football Club had been a client of Flight's taxi service for around 20 years. In 1957 the company was privileged to transport the triumphant team, by coach, on a parade throughout the streets of central Birmingham after they beat Manchester United 2 – 1 to win the FA Cup. This lead to Flights regularly providing a coach to transport the team to certain away matches – an arrangement that continues to this day by the Flights-Hallmark business.

In 1960 a new AEC Reliance with Harrington Cavalier body was purchased which was fitted with just 25 Chapman reclining seats and four tables – enabling 16 passengers to be seated at a table. This was probably the one of the first "executive" type coaches to be operated in Birmingham and was entered by Ken Flight in the 1960 British Coach Rally at Brighton where it was awarded the coveted "Coach of the Year" title.

Coach Cruises were developed in the late 1950's and 1960's and included some quite adventurous destinations. The first continental tour was operated in the early 1960's to Paris and the Loire Valley. The brochure for 1966 included a variety of ever-popular tours to south coast resorts and the Scottish Highlands. If these destinations did not appeal, Scottish Winter Sports breaks to the Ski parks of Blairgowrie or Glenshee were available with daily transport to the ski slopes and skis included.

In April 1961 the business and premises of H Grimsley were acquired. Three Bedford SBs with Duple Vega bodies were included – all except one were disposed of almost immediately. Grimsley's held licences for excursions and summer express services, which would enable further expansion of Flight's programme.

Following this acquisition, the coaches from both fleets were based at the former Grimsley's depot on Berners Street in Lozells. The premises at Victoria Road remained in use as a car sales and service garage with petrol sales forecourt. Agencies were held for the sale of new Rootes group cars and later Ford products. The site was re-developed in the early 1970's with a large showroom built to handle sales of Datsun cars – Japanese vehicles were only just becoming available to the UK in large numbers. This, and another showroom on the Soho Road in Handsworth continued until the mid 1970's.

A further 2 Harrington bodied AEC Reliances were purchased in 1961 and were joined in 1962 by 2 Duple Yeoman bodied Ford Thames. The Fords were acquired with some hesitation owing to the unavailability of Flight's preferred AEC chassis. Both coaches however gave excellent service and based on this experience a further 9 Fords, with Plaxton bodies, were acquired between 1964 and 1967. All, except the last in 1967, were of the longer 36-foot (11 metre) long chassis – some were fitted with Eaton 2-speed axles.

Plaxton bodywork became the standard choice for all purchases from 1963 with a number of AEC Reliances purchased alongside the Fords. Most were acquired new, but in 1966 three one-year-old examples from the Wallace Arnold fleet were acquired. New examples between 1963 and 1966 were of the Panorama design and Flights added the word "Continental" in chrome letters alongside the official model name to distinguish their vehicles from those of competitors.

Two Handsworth based businesses were acquired in 1964; Dalton's and Sugden's. Both companies operated from adjoining premises on the corner of Soho Road and Alfred Road. Only 1 of Sugden's coaches was retained for a short time, but again, valuable licences offered further expansion for Flights. Around this time, Ken Flight established a travel agency located on the Soho Road, where the general public could book British and Foreign travel, as well as Flight's own excursions and coach holidays.

During the 1950's and 1960's Ken Flight was an enthusiastic supporter of both the British and National Coach Rallies held each year at Brighton and Blackpool. The first entry was with Burlingham Seagull bodied AEC Regal, OON 707 at the first British Coach Rally held in Clacton. Subsequent entries at Brighton and Blackpool would see many trophies and awards presented to Flights including the prestigious "Coach of the Year" title as well as Ken Flight winning the Driving Test section in the 1956 "Driver of the Year" competition, in TOB 377. Future such success in Flight's history would give the company, a so far, unequalled 6 such wins at the Brighton event.

A rare vehicle, for an independent operator, was purchased in 1967 in the shape of a Bristol RELH chassis with Plaxton Panorama body. This was the first Bristol to be sold to a private operator – all previous examples being solely for the B.E.T. group. The chassis specification included a Leyland 680 engine, a semi-automatic gearbox and, uncommon for the time, air-suspension. The Plaxton body was

Ken Flight is presented with a trophy by the Mayor of Brighton after winning the Driving Test at the 1956 British Coach Rally. *Ken Flight collection*

built to Flight's high specification, however this impressive vehicle proved troublesome in use and was disliked by drivers.

Following the experience with the Bristol, all future new coaches acquired up to 1972 were Plaxton Elite bodied AEC Reliances – including some early 40-foot long (12 metre) examples. Flights specification included armrests to seats, curtains and even carpets – all items seldom specified by other operators. Additional soundproofing was also installed – providing additional comfort for Flight's passengers.

In 1972 Flights commenced operation of the service between Birmingham city centre and Birmingham (Elmdon Airport). Birmingham City Transport originally provided a bus service but abandoned it in 1964. The route was taken-over in 1964 by Eatonways Coaches who ran it until they ceased to trade in 1968. Den Caney took over from Eatonways but gave up in July 1972, as the route was unprofitable. Flight's were originally granted an Express Service licence but soon applied for stage carriage status – Ken Flight argued that for the route to be profitable, additional pick-up points and intermediate fares were required. A stage carriage licence would also enable bus grants and additional funding to be available. Midland Red, who had services that passed the airport, opposed the application, however Flight's were granted a licence as their service would set-down passengers at the terminal doors, and the vehicles used offered luggage capacity – something that buses used by Midland Red did not.

By the early 1970's the coach fleet had grown to 20 vehicles and licences held to operate summer express services to 11 destinations, and around 300 destinations for excursions and tours. This business had been built up, and flourished throughout the 1950's and 1960's. However Ken Flight observed that by the early 1970's increased car ownership and the availability of package holidays by air, would lead to a downturn in this type of coach travel. Following previously declined offers, Flight's sold their coach business, including 14 coaches, the licences and Berners Street Depot to L F Bowen on 31st October 1973. The fleet continued as a separate operation within the Bowen Group until the late 1970's, by which time Les Bowen had sold his business to the Moseley Group.

From 1974 until 1976 Ken Flight specialised in providing travel and tour packages for UK-bound groups and conference delegates. Mr Flight promoted the business at various trade fairs worldwide arranged by the British Tourist Authority. The Flight's Travel Agency business also continued, and a separate company Flight's Conference Services took advantage of the many opportunities presented with the opening of the National Exhibition Centre.

The break in coach operations was however set to be short lived. With a vision to the future and realising the future increased requirements for air travel, Ken Flight started plans in the mid 1970's for a daily coach service linking Birmingham with London Heathrow Airport… thus a new chapter in the history of Flight's Coach Travel was set to begin.

A Pictorial History of Flights Coaches

The first charabanc operated by Frank Flight was OB 4812 – an ex-Army Austin 2/3 ton van. During the week it served as a van to deliver parcels, furniture and other light goods. *Ken Flight collection*

At weekends a charabanc body with seats for 14 passengers was fitted. OB 4812 is pictured here operating an early pleasure trip – "The Flight Coaches" fleet name can just be made out on the rear of the vehicle. *Ken Flight collection*

Flights – People to Places in Style

Frank Flight is pictured at the wheel of OE 6233, a 1920 Daimler with 24-seat charabanc body. Note that in this view solid tyres are fitted which would restrict the vehicle to a maximum speed of 12 miles per hour. *Ken Flight collection*

A later view of OE 6233 after re-paint into white livery and when fitted with pneumatic tyres – these enabled an increased maximum speed of 20 miles per hour. The passengers' luggage was stored below the floor, however no explanation is available for the suitcase secured to the front mudguard! *Ken Flight collection*

A Pictorial History of Flights Coaches

1924 – AJ 8353, a 1922 Daimler 22hp with 28-seat charabanc body acquired from Robinson, Scarborough. Note that this vehicle has the fleet number "320" and the bird motif painted on the side. *Ken Flight collection*

A rear view of AJ 8353 with a full load of male passengers – Frank Flight is driving. The fleet name and company address can clearly be seen on the rear of the vehicle. *Ken Flight collection*

Flights – People to Places in Style

Another view of AJ 8353 – now fitted with pneumatic tyres. This time it seems that it is the ladies turn for a day out. *Ken Flight collection*

AJ 8353 – pictured on the sea front at Llandudno – long-distance travel 1920's style: over 120 miles from Birmingham. *Ken Flight collection*

A Pictorial History of Flights Coaches

AJ 8353 again working another early pleasure trip. *Ken Flight collection*

1920 – OP 7700, a 14-seat Chevrolet LM – again passengers' luggage is in view, stored below the floor. *Ken Flight collection*

1929 – VP 7882, a Daimler CF6 with elegant looking 32-seat bodywork by Rees and Griffiths.
On this vehicle the bird motif is framed within a triangle with the lettering "The Flight Safety Coaches".
Ken Flight collection

A nearside view of VP 7882. A canvas roof extends as far as the rear axle, with a solid section beyond with luggage storage. *Ken Flight collection*

A Pictorial History of Flights Coaches

VP 7882 pictured on the sea front at Rhyl opposite the "Original Electric Rhyl Rock Factory". The livery is white with black roof and mudguards. Grey is applied to the bonnet and extends to a band below the side windows. *Ken Flight collection*

VP 7882 with DOE 227 behind – a Bedford WTB new in 1937. Note that in this view a solid roof is fitted and the grey band has been extended to form a flare towards the rear of the vehicle. The occasion is an outing arranged by a Handsworth shopkeeper. *Ken Flight collection*

Flights – People to Places in Style

1937 – DOE 227, a Bedford WTB with 26-seat Auto Celulose body – pictured alongside VP 7882. Auto Cellulose were based on Spon Lane in Smethwick and mainly specialised in body repairs although they did build a small number of bodies. *Ken Flight collection*

A rear view of JW 7224 and DOE 227 whilst parked at the rear of the Garage on Victoria Road. *Ken Flight collection*

1946 – JW 7224, a Maudslay SF40 chassis with 35-seat Burlingham body. This vehicle was new in 1935 to Don Everall of Wolverhampton but was acquired by Frank Flight from Turner's of Crowland. *NA3T*

An offside view of JW 7224 – although arguably not one of Burlingham's most attractive designs, this coach worked for Flights until 1952. At some stage a GMC Tank engine was fitted in an effort to overcome the vehicles poor performance on hills. *Ken Flight collection*

1948 – HOL 250, a Maudslay Marathon chassis with 33-seat body built by Santus of Wigan. The coach is pictured at 114 Victoria Road, Aston. *Ken Flight collection*

A partial nearside view of HOL 250. This coach served in the Flight fleet until April 1956. *Ken Flight collection*

A Pictorial History of Flights Coaches

1949 – JOM 797, an Austin CXB chassis with Mann Egerton 31-seat body – other than the full frontal design, the body style resembles the Duple Vista of the period. *Ken Flight collection*

Early business cards issued by Frank Flight.

15

Flights – People to Places in Style

1949 – JVP 700, a 33-seat Windover bodied Maudslay Marathon. Note Frank Flight's initials in chrome letters on the side panels – the bird motif has now been phased out. *Ken Flight collection*

JVP 700 pictured with HOL 250 on the open parking area adjacent to the garage at 114 Victoria Road – this was land acquired after the Second World War. *Ken Flight collection*

An early 1950's view of 114 Victoria Road with JVP 700 and Burlingham Seagull bodied AEC Regal, LOX 700 in view. Note the petrol sales forecourt. *Ken Flight collection*

Coaches parked at the rear of the Victoria Road garage – in view Bedford WTB, DOE 227, Maudslays HOL 250 and JVP 700. *Ken Flight collection*

Flights – People to Places in Style

1951 – LOX 700, a fine looking Burlingham Seagull bodied AEC Regal IV. Driver Phil Smith is pictured with the coach – white coats were standard issue to coach drivers in the 1940's and 1950's. *Ken Flight collection*

A nearside view of LOX 700. This was the first of five Burlingham Seagull bodied AECs operated. One of the most attractive designs of the period, the Seagull was very modern when compared to the half-cab designs that it replaced. *Roy Marshall collection*

A Pictorial History of Flights Coaches

1953 – KDG 523, a 1951 AEC Regal with 37-seat Burlingham Seagull body. Outwardly similar to LOX 700, this coach was acquired from Norton's of Lechlade and was operated until July 1959. *PM Photography*

1954 – OON 707, the second AEC Regal with Burlingham Seagull body acquired new by Flights. Ken Flight is driving whilst competing in the very first British Coach Rally at Clacton. *Roy Marshall collection*

1955 – NOF 550, a 1953 AEC Regal IV with 37-seat Burlingham Seagull body. This coach was acquired from another Birmingham operator – L F Bowen. *K A F Brewin*

Drivers pose for the camera with four Burlingham Seagulls whilst operating a summer express service to Great Yarmouth. All drivers were smartly turned out – those wearing caps had earned the title of "Coach Captain". *Ken Flight collection*

A Pictorial History of Flights Coaches

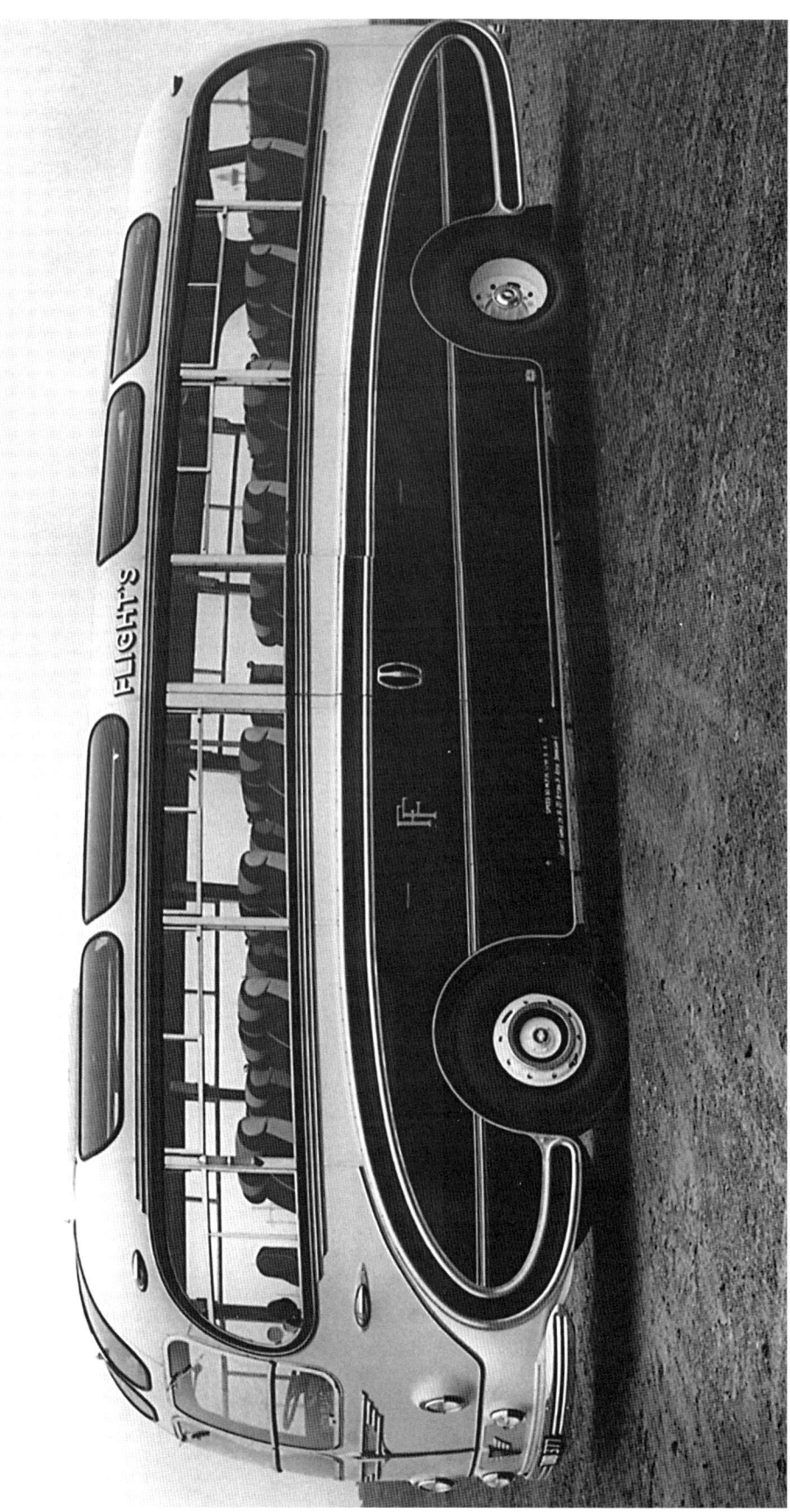

1956 – TOB 377, an AEC Reliance with Burlingham Seagull 37-seat body – the first of many AEC Reliance coaches operated by the company. This coach remained in the fleet until February 1965 but was re-acquired in the late 1990s and completely restored to showroom condition. *Ken Flight collection*

Flights – People to Places in Style

TOB 377 represented Flights at the 1956 British Coach Rally held at Brighton and is pictured here taking part in the road run section of the competition. *Ken Flight collection*

An interior view of TOB 377 – luxury travel 1950's style. *Ken Flight collection*

FLIGHT'S TOURS

Telephone: NOR 0833 & 4309

And Take It From Here

Picking-up Points:
- GARAGE, VICTORIA ROAD, ASTON
- WILLIAM STREET, LOZELLS
- SCOTT ARMS, WALSALL ROAD (North-bound Tours only)

Day and Half-day Tours by Luxury Coaches to the Sea and Country

APRIL 15TH TO MAY 31ST 1956

This Programme will be sent to you each month if you place your name on our mailing list.

Sunday April 15th — A. C.
- Rhyl ... 8-0 16/- 10/9
- Weston ... 8-0 16/9 11/3
- Clevedon ... 8-0 16/9 11/3
- Bristol Zoo ... 8-0 15/- 10/-
- Stratford, Broadway, Evesham ... 2-30 8/- 5/6
- Evening Tour ... 5-30 4/9

Wednesday, April 18th
- Weston ... 8-0 14/- 9/3
- Clevedon ... 8-0 14/- 9/3
- Bristol Zoo ... 8-0 12/6 8/3
- Stratford, Bidford and Alcester ... 2-30 7/6 5/-

Sunday April 22nd
- Rhyl ... 8-0 16/- 11/-
- Weston ... 8-0 16/9 11/3
- Clevedon ... 8-0 16/9 11/3
- Bristol Zoo ... 8-0 15/- 10/-
- Bourton-on-Water ... 2-30 10/6 7/-

Wednesday, April 25th
- Weston ... 8-0 14/- 9/3
- Clevedon ... 8-0 14/- 9/3
- Bristol Zoo ... 8-0 12/6 8/3
- Dovedale Circular ... 2-30 8/9 5/6

Sunday, April 29th
- Sandingham Castle ... 7-30 16/9 11/3
- Weston ... 8-0 16/9 11/3
- Clevedon ... 8-0 16/9 11/3
- Bristol Zoo ... 8-0 15/- 10/-
- Hereford, Tewkesbury and Evesham ... 2-0 10/- 7/6
- Evening Tour ... 5-30 4/9

Wednesday, 2nd May — A.
- Blossom Tour via Worcester, Pershore and Evesham ... 2.30 p.m. 7/6

Saturday, 5th May
- Silverstone Motor Racing inc. admission) ... 7 a.m. 20/-

Sunday, 6th May
- Bournemouth ... 7 a.m. 20/-
- Boscombe ... 7 a.m. 20/-
- Weston ... 8 a.m. 16/9
- Clevedon ... 8 a.m. 16/9
- Bristol Zoo ... 8 a.m. 15/-
- Alton Towers ... 2.30 p.m. 10/-
- Evening Tour ... 5.30 p.m. 4/9

Wednesday, 9th May
- Symonds Yat ... 2 p.m. 10/-
- Blenheim Palace ... 2 p.m. 9/9

Sunday, 13th May
- Rhyl ... 8 a.m. 16/-
- Weston ... 8 a.m. 16/9
- Clevedon ... 8 a.m. 16/9
- Bristol Zoo ... 8 a.m. 15/-
- Bourton-on-the-Water ... 2 p.m. 10/6
- Evening Tour ... 5.30 p.m. 4/9

Wednesday, 16th May
- Rhyl ... 8 a.m. 13/6
- Cwyrich Castle, Colwyn Bay 8 a.m. 15/6
- Blenheim Palace ... 2 p.m. 9/9

Whit Saturday
- Bournemouth ... 7 a.m. 20/-
- Boscombe ... 7 a.m. 20/-
- Weston ... 8 a.m. 16/9
- Bristol Zoo ... 8 a.m. 16/9
- Clevedon ... 8 a.m. 15/-

START OF HOLIDAY SERVICES — EVERY SATURDAY TO THE EAST COAST — ASK FOR LISTS.

Whit Sunday
- Bournemouth ... 7 a.m. 23/3
- Boscombe ... 7 a.m. 23/3
- Weston ... 8 a.m. 18/9
- Clevedon ... 8 a.m. 18/9
- Bristol Zoo ... 8 a.m. 17/-
- Bourton-on-the-Water ... 2 p.m. 11/9
- Evening Tour ... 5.30 p.m. 5/3

Whit Monday
- Bournemouth ... 7 a.m. 23/3
- Southport ... 8 a.m. 18/9
- Burnham-on-Sea ... 8 a.m. 18/9

Whit Tuesday
- Bournemouth ... 7 a.m. 23/3
- Boscombe ... 7 a.m. 23/3
- Rhyl ... 8 a.m. 18/-
- Symonds Yat ... 10 a.m. 13/6
- Dovedale ... 2 p.m. 11/9

Whit Wednesday
- Weston ... 8 a.m. 14/-
- Clevedon ... 8 a.m. 14/-
- Bristol Zoo ... 8 a.m. 12/6
- Windsor and Thames Valley 8 a.m. 14/-
- Blenheim Palace ... 2 p.m. 9/9

Whit Thursday
- Rhyl ... 8 a.m. 13/6
- Ludlow and Church Stretton 2.30 p.m. 8/9

Sunday, 27th May
- Bournemouth ... 7 a.m. 20/-
- Boscombe ... 7 a.m. 20/-
- Mablethorpe ... 8 a.m. 18/9
- Sutton-on-Sea ... 8 a.m. 18/9
- The Beautiful Hoar Cross Country in Blythfield Dam 2.30 p.m. 10/-
- Evening Tour ... 5.30 p.m. 4/9

Tuesday, 29th May
- New Brighton via Tunnel ... 8 a.m. 14/-
- Dovedale ... 2 p.m. 8/-

Wednesday, 30th May
- Burnham-on-Sea ... 8 a.m. 14/-
- Bristol Zoo ... 8 a.m. 12/6
- Compton Wynyates ... 2.30 p.m. 8/-

Thursday, 31st May
- Aberdovey ... 8 a.m. 14/-
- Towyn-on-Sea ... 8 a.m. 14/6
- Malvern Circular ... 2.30 p.m. 7/6

TOURS TO THE SEA & COUNTRY EVERY DAY DURING SUMMER MONTHS. Ask for Monthly Programme.

PRIVATE HIRE — VERY LATEST TYPE LUXURY RADIO & HEATED COACHES FOR ALL OCCASIONS. BROCHURE ON REQUEST

SUMMER HOLIDAY SERVICES FOR 1956

GREAT YARMOUTH, LOWESTOFT, CAISTER-ON-SEA, CORTON-ON-SEA, GORLESTON-ON-SEA, HOPTON-ON-SEA, GUNTON HALL HOLIDAY CAMP, EASTBOURNE, BOURNEMOUTH, RHYL, COLWYN BAY AND LLANDUDNO

For fare times and picking-up points see Express Service Lists

Please Book in Advance at:—
HEAD OFFICE OR AGENTS IN LOCAL AREAS
FLIGHTS GARAGE LTD., 114-120 VICTORIA ROAD, ASTON 'Phones: NOR 0833 or 4309

E. H. Russell & Co., Ltd. Printers, 1 Park Lane, Aston 6

Licences were held by the company to operate Day excursions. This leaflet advertises the trips available for April and May in 1956.

Flights – People to Places in Style

"Take it from here and let yourself go with Flight's Tours."

A late 1950's brochure for private hire organisers – a guide listing over 100 suggested itineraries for day and half-day trips to the coast, countryside and combined land and river cruises.

A late 1950's view of 114 Victoria Road, Aston with all five Burlingham Seagull bodied AEC coaches in view. Note the chalkboards outside the booking office advertising forthcoming trips. *Ken Flight collection*

As well as the garage and booking office for the coach fleet, the site also incorporated a petrol sales forecourt and car sales show room. *Ken Flight collection*

Flights – People to Places in Style

In 1957 Aston Villa beat Manchester United 2-1 to win the FA Cup, and Flight's were hired to transport the victorious team on a parade through central Birmingham. In this view LOX 700 is turning on to Colmore Row by the original Snow Hill station. *Ken Flight collection*

LOX 700 heads along Colmore Row towards Victoria Square with TOB 377 and OON 707 following. *Ken Flight collection*

A Pictorial History of Flights Coaches

Thousands cheered the team as the procession made its way along Colmore Row. *Ken Flight collection*

Flights – People to Places in Style

1960 – 477 AOP, an AEC Reliance with Harrington Cavalier body is pictured outside the AEC offices in Southall. This was the first of three such vehicles acquired new. *Andrew Roberts collection*

When new, 477 AOP was fitted with just 25 seats and four tables and in this set-up would be used to transport the Aston Villa team to certain away matches. It is pictured here on Madeira Drive in Brighton whilst taking part in the 1960 British Coach Rally. Note the "Flights Tours" fleet name appearing in chrome letters on the side of the coach. *R H G Simpson*

Ken Flight manoeuvres 477 AOP during the driving tests at the British Coach Rally – Mr Flight was "runner-up coach driver of the year". *Ken Flight collection*

A rear view of the coach on Madeira Drive – the fleet name is displayed on flags on the boot doors – a new feature introduced to coincide with the "Cavalier" theme. *Ken Flight collection*

Flights – People to Places in Style

Success for Flight's Tours – 477 AOP is awarded the "Coach of the Year" title at Brighton. Decorated with floral garlands, the coach is proudly driven by Ken Flight to the awards presentation area. *Ken Flight collection*

Left to right – Mrs Gwen Flight, Ken Flight, Ken Flight's sister Marjorie, nephew John and driver Bob Porch collect the "Coach of the Year" trophy and other silverware. *Ken Flight collection*

A Pictorial History of Flights Coaches

Upon return to Birmingham, 477 AOP and its awards are posed in Front of Aston Hall. This coach was operated until 1966 but was later re-acquired in 1988 and restored. Although no longer owned by the Flight family it is still preserved in Flight's Tour livery. *Ken Flight collection*

An interior view of 477 AOP – the seats are Chapman recliners fitted in place of the standard Harrington fixed units. Tables and smart white headrest covers add to the quality of presentation. *Ken Flight collection*

FLIGHT'S TOURS ARE PLEASED TO ANNOUNCE
THAT WE HAVE TAKEN OVER . . .

Grimsleys Coaches and Garage
207-213, Berners Street, Lozells

IT HAS NOW BEEN ALTERED
AND DECORATED TO BECOME
The Coach Station, Lozells

ALL OUR COACHES ARE NOW
BASED AND SERVICED THERE

FLIGHT'S TOURS, VICTORIA ROAD, IS
THE HEAD OFFICE AND CHART ROOM

Bookings can be made at Agents or :
FLIGHT'S TOURS LTD.,
114-120, Victoria Road, Aston
EASt 3592 (4 lines)
FLIGHT'S TOURS LTD. COACH STATION
205-213, Berners Street, Lozells   NOR 0941

FLIGHTS Tours

THROUGHOUT ENGLAND SCOTLAND WALES

For Your Next Holiday

Also Easter and Whitsun Tours

An announcement was published (above) to inform patrons of the acquisition of Grimsley's Coaches and Garage in Lozells. Although the premises on Victoria Road in Aston remained the company's head office, all coaches were transferred to the former Grimsley's garage on Berners Street in Lozells. Flights were also keen to inform potential customers of their success at the 1960 Coach Rally (below).

1961 brochure for Coach Cruises, Excursions and summer Coach Services (above) – despite the introduction of the Harrington bodied coaches the design of the front cover was carried over from previous editions and featured an impression of a Burlingham Seagull.

★ We are PROUD TO ANNOUNCE that at the

1960 BRITISH COACH RALLY

FLIGHT'S TOURS Ltd. WON THE TOP AWARDS CUPS

1st Concours d'Elegance

1st Driving Tests

1st Best Vehicle in its Class

1st Best Entered Harrington Body

Awards were also won by our vehicles in the 1956 Coach Rally.

A Pictorial History of Flights Coaches

1961 – The business of H Grimsley of Lozells, Birmingham was acquired. Three Bedford SBs with Duple Vega bodies were acquired including TOF 3, which was new in 1956 and remained with Flights until March 1963. *Roy Marshall collection*

Two more new Harrington Cavalier bodied AEC Reliances joined the fleet in 1961 – 577 DOG seated 41 passengers and was the first to enter service in February of that year. *R H G Simpson*

1961 – the second new Harrington bodied AEC this year was 677 DOF which is pictured here when new en-route to Brighton whilst competing in the British Coach Rally. *Ken Flight collection*

On Madeira Drive, Ken Flight pilots 677 DOF through the driving tests. As with 477 AOP the previous year just 25 seats are fitted and four tables. The lettering on the boot doors has been changed to read "Flight's Tours, Aston and Lozells". *Ken Flight collection*

Flights high standards of presentation are rewarded with more silver ware for 1961. Left to right – Ken Flight, Bill Baller (General Manager and Director), Ken Flight's sister Marjorie and Mrs Gwen Flight. *Ken Flight collection*

677 DOF took over as the team coach for Aston Villa from 477 AOP. Upon return from the British Coach Rally, the coach is posed with its awards at Villa Park. *Ken Flight collection*

Flights – People to Places in Style

SERVICE No. 1A.
GREAT YARMOUTH
WEEKLY AND FORTNIGHTLY BOOKINGS

Depart: Flight's Tours Ltd., Victoria Rd...... 6.15 a.m.
         Handsworth, Regal Cinema .... 6.20 a.m.
         Hamstead, Beaufort Inn .... 6.25 a.m.
         Great Barr, Scott Arms .... 6.28 a.m.
         Kingstanding Circle .... 6.33 a.m.
         Erdington 'Bus Terminus .... 6.37 a.m.
         Sutton Coldfield, W. H. Smith's ...... 6.42 a.m.
Returning from Coach Station, Beaconsfield Road at 2.40 p.m. or 3.36 p.m.
FARES: ADULTS - 42/-   CHILDREN 21/-
        Peak Holiday Weeks 45/-   22/6

SERVICE No. 2B.
GREAT YARMOUTH
WEEKLY AND FORTNIGHTLY BOOKINGS

Depart: Flight's Tours Ltd., Victoria Rd...... 6.32 a.m.
         Erdington 'Bus Terminus .... 6.37 a.m.
         Sutton Parade, W. H. Smith's .... 6.42 a.m.
Returning from Coach Station, Beaconsfield Road at 2.40 p.m. or 3.36 p.m.
FARES: ADULTS - 42/-   CHILDREN 21/-
        Peak Holiday Weeks 45/-   22/6

SERVICE No. 3A.
LOWESTOFT
WEEKLY AND FORTNIGHTLY BOOKINGS

Depart: Flight's Tours Ltd., Victoria Rd...... 6.15 a.m.
         Handsworth, Regal Cinema .... 6.20 a.m.
         Hamstead, Beaufort Inn .... 6.25 a.m.
         Great Barr, Scott Arms .... 6.28 a.m.
         Kingstanding Circle .... 6.33 a.m.
         Erdington 'Bus Terminus .... 6.37 a.m.
         Sutton Coldfield, W. H. Smith's ..
Returning from Lowestoft Coach Park
FARES: ADULTS - 44/3   C
        Peak Holiday Weeks 47/3

SERVICE No. 4A.
CORTON-ON-SEA
WEEKLY AND FORTNIGHTLY B

Depart: Flight's Tours Ltd., Victoria Rd..
         Handsworth, Regal Cinema .....
         Hamstead, Beaufort Inn ....
         Great Barr, Scott Arms ....
         Kingstanding Circle ....
         Erdington 'Bus Terminus ......
         Sutton Coldfield, W. H. Smith's .
Returning from the Hut Hotel at 3.1
FARES: ADULTS - 44/3   C
        Peak Holiday Weeks 47/3

Note: This Service is most convenient for pa at Corton Beach, Warners and Holiday Camps.

Extracts from the 1961 brochure – licences were held to operate summer coach services to popular holiday resorts. Demand for such services remained high throughout the 1960's and early 1970's until private car ownership increased.

SCOTTISH LOCHS & CENTRAL HIGHLANDS
SEVEN DAYS

1st Day. We commence our Tour at 9 o'clock and go out to Tamworth and on to Ashby-de-la-Zouch for Morning Coffee.
On to Long Eaton, Nottingham, Mansfield, Ollerton, Bawtry to Doncaster for lunch to be served.
Leaving Doncaster we go on to Wetherby Knaresborough, to Boroughbridge for afternoon tea.
Proceeding on to Leeming Bar, Catterick to Darlington where we stay for dinner, bed and breakfast.

2nd Day. Leaving after breakfast we go out via Spennymoor, Gateshead Newcastle-upon-Tyne to Otterburn for morning coffee.
On to Hawick for lunch to be served.
Leaving for Galashields, Lauder, so to Eddleston where we stay for tea, dinner, bed and breakfast.

3rd Day. We leave after breakfast for Edinburgh, and on the way visit the world famous Forth Bridge and Edinburgh Castle. We stay for lunch, dinner, bed and breakfast. This gives the afternoon free for sightseeing.
As Edinburgh is Scotland's Capital and University City, there are many places of interest to visit. Two of its noted attractions are the delightful Prince's St. Gardens and the famous Floral Clock. Edinburgh is also associated with Mary Queen of Scots and Darnley.

4th Day. We leave for Stirling for morning coffee.
On to Dryman, Loch Lomond, to Balloch for lunch to be served.
Proceeding on to Inversnaid, Crainlarich, Lochernhead, Leny Falls, Callender back to Stirling for afternoon tea.
We then leave and go back to Edinburgh for dinner, bed and breakfast

5th Day. Leaving after breakfast we proceed out via Peebles, Tweedsmuir over the Devil's Beef Tub to Moffat, which is associated with the Poet Robert Burns, for lunch to be served.
On to Locherbie, Ecclefechan to Gretna Green, which was famous for its runaway marriages, for afternoon tea.
Proceeding on to Windermere where we have dinner, bed and breakfast.

6th Day.   A CLEAR DAY IN WINDERMERE
           ALL MEALS TO BE TAKEN AT THE HOTEL

7th Day. Leaving the Hotel after breakfast we proceed out to Kendal Carnforth, Lancaster to Preston for morning coffee.
On to Wigan, Warrington, Knutsford to lunch to be served.
Then we go on to Holmes Chaple, Newcastle-under-Lyme to Stafford for afternoon tea.
On to Birmingham and arriving in at approximately 6.30 p.m.

DEPARTURE DATES and INCLUSIVE FARES UPON APPLICATION

A selection of "Coach Cruises" featured tours to the Scottish Highlands – a speciality of Flights.

A 1961 view of the Berners Street garage with Harrington Cavalier bodied AEC Reliances 677 DOF, 577 DOG and 477 AOP in view. In common with the coach fleet, the company premises were presented to a very high standard. *Ken Flight collection*

1962 – Two Ford Thames 570E chassis with 41-seat Duple Yeoman bodies were acquired this year including 877 FOH pictured here inside the Berners Street garage. *Colin Ludford*

A nearside view of 877 FOH – this coach was delivered with registration number 206 BLA – having been used by the supplying dealer as a demonstration vehicle prior to entering service with Flights. *R H G Simpson*

32 BCG was the second of the pair and had been new the previous year to Banstead Coaches. Both vehicles were operated by Flights until January 1966. *Colin Ludford*

A Pictorial History of Flights Coaches

Berners Street depot – circa 1962. Left to right: 477 AOP, 577 DOG – driver Charlie Day, 677 DOF – driver John Brookes, 777 FOH – driver Bob Porch, 877 FOH – driver Don Jevons and 32 BCG.
Ken Flight collection

Flights – People to Places in Style

1962 – The AEC Reliance remained Flight's choice for chassis but the Plaxton Panorama body was chosen for this year's new purchase. 777 FOH is pictured when new at the British Coach Rally in Brighton. The longer length of 36 foot allowed 39-seats and six tables to be fitted. The model name "Panorama" can bee seen in chrome letters below the first side window – Flights also added "Continental" in identical style. *Ken Flight collection*

A rear view of 777 FOH – amongst additional features specified by Flights is the additional bright trim along the length of the vehicle. *Ken Flight collection*

An interior view of 777 FOH – the headrests on this vehicle are believed to be to Flight's own specification. *Ken Flight collection*

Ken Flight in the driving seat of 777 FOH – with a fine display of cups awarded at the Coach Rallies at Blackpool and Brighton – including the 1962 "Coach of the Year" at Brighton. This picture also provides an excellent view of the driver's area of a 1960's touring coach – a vast improvement from the half-cab designs of the 1940's and 1950's. *Ken Flight collection*

Flights – People to Places in Style

1963 – 977 JOB another Plaxton Panorama bodied AEC Reliance – the only new coach purchased this year. The destination display is lettered for Aston Villa Football Club – note the unusual fleet name style in this view. *Roy Marshall collection*

Another view of 977 JOB pictured beside 747 MOH – one of four Plaxton bodied Ford Thames purchased new in 1964. 977 JOB had a short life in the fleet – unfortunately it was destroyed by fire after being hit by a car in 1965. *R H G Simpson*

1964 – 737 MOB, a Ford Thames 676E chassis with 51-seat Plaxton Panorama body – one of four delivered new this year. *Pete Southern collection*

707 MOP was delivered in May 1964 and was the last of the quartet to enter service. These vehicles were acquired following successful operation of the Duple bodied Thames coaches purchased in 1962. *Colin Ludford*

Flights – People to Places in Style

1964 – 717 MOB, an AEC Reliance with Plaxton Panorama body was another new coach acquired this year. Fitted with 37 seats and tables, the coach is pictured at a wet British Coach Rally in Brighton.
Ken Flight collection

Ken Flight gently manoeuvres the coach through a narrow gate during the coach driving competition.
Ken Flight collection

A Pictorial History of Flights Coaches

Receiving silver cups at Brighton 1964 – left to right: driver Bob Porch, actress Dora Bryan, Ken Flight, Mrs Gwen Flight and driver Charlie Day. *Ken Flight collection*

Back at Berners Street – 717 MOB and 727 MOB display their cups awarded at the 1964 Coach Rally. The view allows comparison of the different frontal styling of the Plaxton Panorama body when fitted to different chassis. The front position of the engine of the Ford chassis required the large oval grill and re-positioning of the destination box. *Ken Flight collection*

Flights – People to Places in Style

Ford Thames, 727 MOB was also entered in the 1963 British Coach Rally – it is pictured here on Madeira Drive with drivers Eric Jennings and Don Jevons. The highly polished paintwork would no doubt of added a few points when judged in the "Concours d'Elegance". *Ken Flight collection*

A rear view of 727 MOB showing the revised boot door sign writing introduced in 1964. *Ken Flight collection*

A Pictorial History of Flights Coaches

Dora Bryan presenting awards to Ken Flight at Brighton in 1963 – this time the cups are for 727 MOB. Left to right: Drivers Eric Jennings, Don Jevons, Dora Bryan, Ken Flight and General Manager, and Director, Bill Baller – affectionately known as "the Station Master". *Ken Flight collection*

Flights – People to Places in Style

1965 – Four more Plaxton bodied Fords were added to the fleet this year – all had Plaxton's revised Panorama design and were built upon Ford's latest R-series chassis. COL 787C is pictured here prior to delivery. *Ken Flight collection*

An interior view of COL 787C when fitted with 37 seats and 6 tables – the seat moquette was simulation ocelot skin, this and window curtains were new for 1965 and would become standard for new purchases over the next few years. *Ken Flight collection*

Rally success again for Flight's Tours – COL 787C was awarded the "Coach of the Year" title at the British Coach Rally, Brighton. *Ken Flight collection*

The Flight family, with their collection of awarded cups and trophies, pose for the camera at Brighton – left to right: Geoff Flight, Ken Flight, Mrs Gwen Flight and Sheila Anne Flight. The awards included "Coach of the Year", the Alf Moseley trophy, Ford trophy, Plaxton trophy and highest placed operator (under 50 vehicles fleet). *Ken Flight collection*

Flights – People to Places in Style

Flights sent a second entry to the 1965 British Coach Rally – COL 797C pictured here on Madeira Drive looking pristine. *Ken Flight collection*

A rear view of COL 797C – this coach was to standard specification with 52 seats fitted and won the "Top Touring Coach" award. *Ken Flight collection*

A Pictorial History of Flights Coaches

Pictured when returning from a day excursion to North Wales, driver Ron Allen is seen with the third of the 1965 Ford-Plaxtons – COL 767C. *Colin Ludford*

The last of the new coaches delivered in 1965 was COM 777C. This coach entered service in May of this year and was operated until February 1970. *PM Photography*

Flights – People to Places in Style

1966 Tours programme. This included popular holidays to South Coast British resorts and Scottish touring holidays. A novel feature was also the inclusion of Scottish Winter Sports breaks in January and February – these were based at Glenshee and were available for 3, 5 and 8-days duration.

A Pictorial History of Flights Coaches

1966 – Three Plaxton bodied AEC Reliances were acquired in February – all had been new the previous year to Wallace Arnold Tours. BNW 627C was one of two 51-seaters – note in this view that there is no black around the front screen or side windows – this was added at a later date. *R H G Simpson*

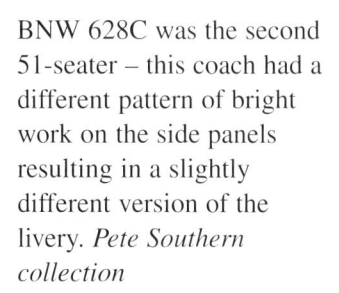

BNW 628C was the second 51-seater – this coach had a different pattern of bright work on the side panels resulting in a slightly different version of the livery. *Pete Southern collection*

The third ex Wallace Arnold coach was CUM 533C – a 43-seater. Former Flights driver, Pete Southern, recalls that this coach "went like a rocket". *P M Photography*

53

Two new AEC Reliances with Plaxton Panorama bodies were also purchased in 1966. FOP 701D is pictured prior to delivery – note that the ribbed trim around the front windows has been altered – also the fleet name is now displayed on illuminated panels on the front and sides of the coach. *Ken Flight collection*

An interior view of FOP 701D shows the additional items specified by Flights: arm rests to the seats, curtains and a gangway carpet. *Ken Flight collection*

FOP 702D was the second new AEC – Plaxton and is seen here in a publicity photograph for AEC. *Ken Flight collection*

When new FOP 702D was fitted with reduced seating and tables and in this set-up would perform executive hires and carry the Aston Villa Football team to away matches. *Ken Flight collection*

Flights – People to Places in Style

FOP 701D and FOP 702D were both entered in the 1966 National Coach Rally at Blackpool, and the British Coach Rally at Brighton. Both are pictured here at Brighton whilst being inspected by the Judges in the Concours d'elegance. *Ken Flight collection*

The exceptional presentation of Flight's vehicles earned the company many awards at the coach rallies. 1966 was no exception and in this view drivers Ricky Ions, Brian Richardson and Eddie Knowles are pictured receiving cups from the Mayor of Brighton. *Ken Flight collection*

A Pictorial History of Flights Coaches

FOP 702D and FOP 701D are displayed at Aston Hall with their collection of awards from the Brighton and Blackpool coach rallies. FOP 701D: Highest placed standard coach (Blackpool and Brighton), Chapman trophy (Brighton). FOP 702D: Runner-up at Blackpool and Brighton, Plaxton trophy, Associated Weavers trophy – best interior décor and smartest crew award. *Ken Flight collection*

Left to right: John Rowlands, Ricky Ions, Ken Flight, Ken Sutton and Bob Porch. *Ken Flight collection*

Flights – People to Places in Style

1967 – Two new coaches joined the fleet this year, the first was JON 700E a Bristol RELH chassis with Plaxton Panorama I body. The coach is pictured at Brighton where it was awarded the highest placed standard coach award, the Arlington trophy and smartest uniformed driver award. *Ken Flight collection*

The coach had a Leyland 680 engine, a semi-automatic gearbox and air suspension and was the first Bristol to be delivered to an independent. Despite the high specification it proved troublesome in operation and was disliked by drivers, however it was kept in the fleet until 1971. *Andrew Roberts collection*

A Pictorial History of Flights Coaches

The second new coach in 1967 was KOE 703E, a Ford with 45-seat Plaxton Panorama I body. This was the last Ford purchased and the only example of the shorter R192 chassis operated. *Photobus*

JON 700E pictured next to Flights Travel Agency in Handsworth with chalkboards advertising Evening Tours. *Pete Southern collection*

Flights – People to Places in Style

In the 1960's, a travel agency located at 272 Soho Road was established. This was a full ABTA bonded outlet offering international and domestic travel and holiday reservations as well as bookings for Flight's own coach holidays and excursions. The Austin Mini Traveller was used to deliver travel tickets to clients.
Ken Flight collection

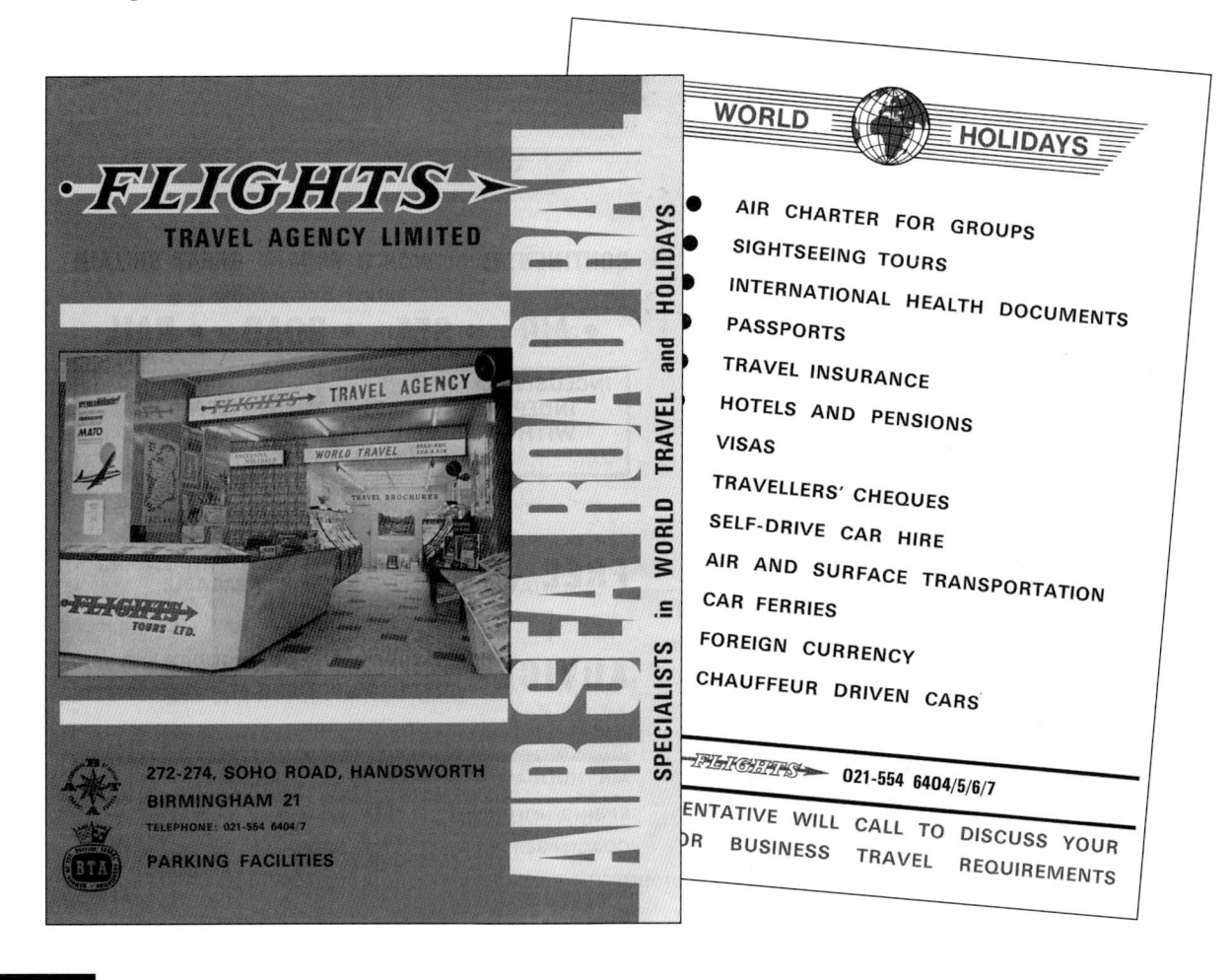

A Pictorial History of Flights Coaches

An interior view of the Travel Agency office – as with all parts of the Flight business this was smartly presented. *Ken Flight collection*

The adjacent premises were used by Flight's Garages as a car showroom – note that the upper parts of the building have been deleted in this publicity photograph. *Ken Flight collection*

1968 brochure for coach excursions – Flights were one of the major operators of day trips, and summer coastal services from Birmingham. A number of pick-up points were authorised to the company in the North West of the city.

1969 – Two new coaches were purchased this year – both AEC Reliances with the latest Plaxton Panorama Elite body. ROE 704G was the first and is pictured here in Blackpool. *PM Photography*

A near side picture of ROE 704G – the bright trim along the side of these coaches was modified to accommodate Flight's livery requirements – note also the additional indicators and roof marker lights. *Andrew Roberts collection*

ROE 705G was the second of the 1969 AEC – Plaxtons and is pictured here whilst parked inside the garage at Berners Street. With destination sign set, a reduced seating capacity and tables fitted, the coach is prepared to transport the Aston Villa team on another away fixture. *Colin Ludford*

ROE 704G arrives at Victoria Square, Birmingham with the Aston Villa team – possibly on the occasion of the team winning the 3rd Division Championship for the 1971 / 72 season. *Ken Flight collection*

1969 brochure for coach cruises and summer holiday services.

PANORAMIC COACHES FOR PRIVATE HIRE

Our fleet of Luxury Pullman coaches is a[vailable for] Private Hire in the United Kingdom and on the [Continent] of Europe for all occasions at competitive rates.

Coach travel at its best, with panoramic v[iews for] passengers, luxuriously upholstered with ind[ividual] rests, including the back rows. Each vehicle [is fitted] with radio and heaters, and individual passe[nger] ventilation. Coaches entered by FLIGHT'S T[ravel] have won major awards in British and Intern[ational] Rallies, competing against the finest coa[ches in the] country and the Continent. You can hir[e these] winning coaches at no extra cost, and enjoy [the knowledge] that your party is having the best conveya[nce] for their outing.

The success of any organised tour depends on first-class coaches and drivers, and careful attention to a detailed itinerary. Our private Hire Department is under personal supervision and specialises in arranging itineraries for parties large and small. Organisers can rely on excellent catering arrangements, theatre reservations, sea and river trips, hotel accommodation, etc., all free of any booking charges.

We await your enquiries—quotations are given immediately!

Coach Cruises & FLIGHTS Holiday Services 1969

The brochure also advertised the company's private hire service.

Flights – People to Places in Style

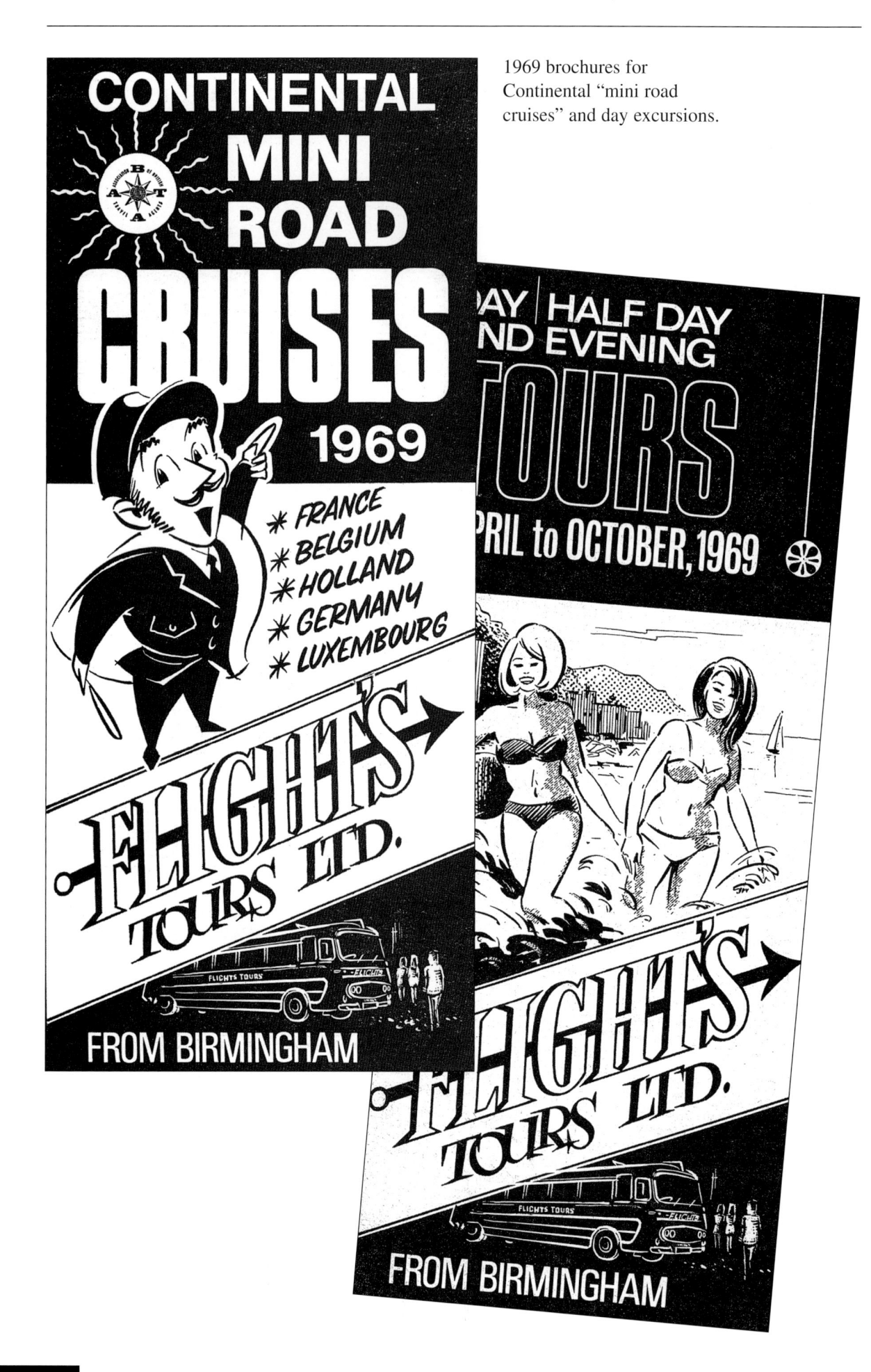

1969 brochures for Continental "mini road cruises" and day excursions.

A Pictorial History of Flights Coaches

1970 – Three more Plaxton Panorama Elite bodied AEC Reliances are acquired. UOM 707H was the first of the three and was also the first 40ft (12-metre) coach to join the fleet. The extra long body enabled 55 passenger seats. *R H G Simpson*

The other two 1970 AECs were 11-metre examples with seats for 51 passengers. UOM 709H was the last of the three to be registered. *Daniel Hill collection*

Flights – People to Places in Style

1970 brochure for coach excursions.

1971 – Three brand new Plaxton bodied AEC Reliances joined the fleet this year – all were 12-metre examples with 57 seats. YOB 720J is pictured in Great Yarmouth with passengers and luggage being loaded for the return to Birmingham. *Andrew Roberts collection*

Also pictured in Great Yarmouth is YOB 730J – all three coaches had Plaxton's Elite II body. A fourth coach, YOB 710J, also entered the fleet – this was the chassis of 717 MOB with a new body to the shorter length of 11-metres. *Andrew Roberts collection*

Flights – People to Places in Style

Driver George Doidge and Ken Flight with 1971 AEC Reliance – Plaxton, YOB 740J. *Ken Flight collection*

HIRE YOUR COACH FROM FLIGHTS TOURS LTD.

HANDBOOK FOR PRIVATE HIRE

94 COTSWOLDS
The delightful scenery of the Cotswolds with its Hills, Dales and Villages is in great demand. Via Stratford, Shipston-on-Stour, Stow-on-the-Wold, Bourton-on-the-Water (Lunch), Burford, Bibury, Cirencester, Birdlip, Cheltenham (Tea), Evesham, Redditch. 160 *miles*

95 COTSWOLDS
Another Cotswold Tour covering many interesting points. Stratford, Moreton-in-the-Marsh, Stow-on-the-Wold, Bourton-on-the-Water, Northleach, Cirencester, Cheltenham, Evesham, Redditch. 146 *miles*

96 COTSWOLDS (Lesser known villages)
A quiet country tour of great beauty, very popular. Via Stratford, Mickleton, Chipping Campden, Blockley, Bourton-on-the-Hill, Moreton-in-Marsh, Stow-on-the-Wold, Ford, Stanway, Stanton, Broadway, Evesham, Redditch. 103 *miles*

97 COTSWOLDS EDGE
This tour follows the edge of the Cotswold Hills. Stratford, Shipston-on-Stour, Long Compton, Chipping Norton, Burford, Cirencester, Stroud, Painswick, Cheltenham, Winchcombe, Broadway, Bidford, Alcester.

98 CRANHAM WOODS
One of the loveliest spots on the edge of the Cotswolds. Glorious views. Via Evesham, Winchcombe, Cheltenham, Birdlip, Cranham. Visit Prinknash Abbey. Return via Painswick, Gloucester, Tewkesbury, Upton-on-Severn, Powick, Holt Fleet, Ombersley. 112 *miles*

99 DODINGTON HOUSE & PARK
This stately home adorned by two picturesque lakes and magnificent Park is very popular with our patrons, and can be included in any of our tours going south to the Bath or Bristol areas. Excellent catering facilities. 162 *miles*

100 DOVEDALE
Ideal tour for hikers, beautiful hills and dales. Via Lichfield, Kings Bromley, Sudbury, Ashbourne, Ilam. Return via Ashbourne, Rocester, Uttoxeter, Blythfield Reservoir, Rugeley, Lichfield. 110 *miles*

101 DRAYTON MANOR PARK
Inland pleasure resort, many interesting features. Excellent catering. Via Curdworth, Marston. Return same route. 30 *miles*

19

1970's Private Hire handbook – a 42-page book produced for party organisers that featured over 160 suggested tours and visits.

70

A Pictorial History of Flights Coaches

Berners Street depot – circa 1971 with Plaxton bodied AEC Reliances from 1969, 1970 and 1971 in view. Left to right: ROE 705G, UOM 707H, YOB 710J, ROE704G, UOM 708H and YOB 730J. The chassis of YOB 710J was originally 717 MOB – the original body was destroyed by fire in 1965. *Ken Flight collection*

Flights – People to Places in Style

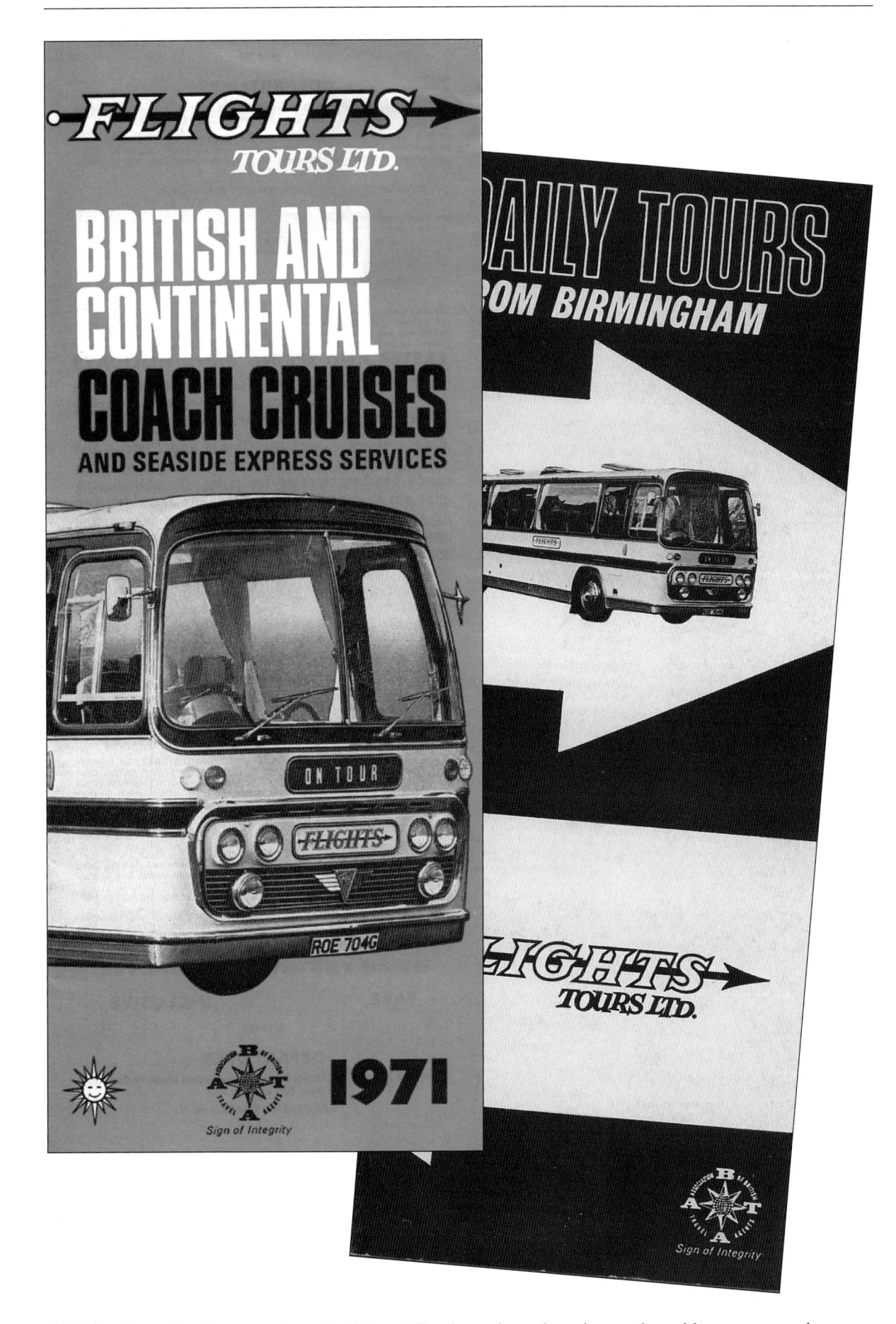

1971 brochures for day excursions, British and Continental coach cruises and seaside express services.

A Pictorial History of Flights Coaches

The three Harrington Cavalier bodied AECs brought new by Flights had all left the fleet by 1966, however five examples dating from 1960 were acquired in 1971. All were new to Greenslades Tours, Exeter. 557 AFJ is pictured following re-paint into Flight's livery. *Daniel Hill collection*

558 AFJ – another of the ex-Greenslades Harringtons – these coaches were additional fleet vehicles and, despite their 11 years of age, looked just as smart as all Flight's other coaches. *Andrew Roberts collection*

Flights – People to Places in Style

1972 – Two further 12-metre Plaxton Panorama Elite II bodied AEC Reliances were purchased this year. CVP 770K represented the company at the British Coach Rally in Brighton. *Ken Flight collection*

Receiving cups at Brighton for CVP 770K – including the highest placed standard coach, the Plaxton trophy and Kirkby trophy. Left to right: Driver George Doidge, the Mayor and Mayoress of Brighton, Ken Flight and driver Malcolm Griffith. *Ken Flight collection*

A Pictorial History of Flights Coaches

CVP 770K photographed at Aston Hall upon return from the coach rally. This view shows clearly the revised side mouldings specified by Flights for their 1971 and 1972 deliveries. Plaxton adopted this style as standard for the Elite III when introduced for the 1973 season. *Ken Flight collection*

A totally immaculate presentation was the hallmark of Flight's vehicles – note also the temporary replacement windscreen (laminated screens had yet to become available). It's no surprise that Flight's won so many awards at the coach rallies over the years. *Ken Flight collection*

Flights – People to Places in Style

An interior view of Plaxton Elite II bodied AEC – CVP 770K. *Ken Flight collection*

CVP 750K was the other new coach delivered in 1972 and is pictured here in Lozells, Birmingham. *Daniel Hill collection*

A Pictorial History of Flights Coaches

Aston Hall in Birmingham forms the backdrop for this picture, which has all of the Plaxton Elite II bodied AEC Reliances from 1971 and 1972 in view. *Ken Flight collection*

Flights – People to Places in Style

An early 1970's view of the Victoria Road, Aston garage. The original garage, and acquired properties either side, have been cleared and a new petrol sales forecourt and sales showroom erected. *Ken Flight collection*

An interior view of the new car showroom with a full range of Datsun cars displayed. Flight's Garage was one of the first agencies in Birmingham to sell Japanese cars, which were still relatively uncommon at the time. *Ken Flight collection*

1973 brochure for Continental coach cruises and Express services.

Day excursions brochure 1973 – the last year that Flights would operate day excursions as the licences held, and the coach fleet, were sold to L F Bowen at the end of the 1973 season.

Flights – People to Places in Style

As well as taking part in the British Coach Rally at Brighton, Flight's also regularly attended the National Coach Rally at Blackpool, 677 DOF is pictured at the 1961 event.

Timetable for the Birmingham Airport Coach Service – circa 1973 – this route was the forerunner to the "Flightlink" services.

Part Two: 1977-2002 onwards

In June 1977, three Plaxton Viewmaster bodied Leyland Leopard coaches took to the streets of Birmingham. Painted cream and black and adorned with additional chrome trim and marker lights, these vehicles were reminiscent of the Flight's Tours coaches, but had the fleet name "Forward Coaches".

The sale agreement with L F Bowen in 1973 prevented the Flight name being used until 1979 – "Forward" being the motto of the City of Birmingham, and displayed on its coat of arms. Two further Viewmasters were delivered in August 1977 with "S" registration marques and these five impressive vehicles formed the Flight family's re-entry into coach operation.

The new operation began operating from the former Dalton and Sugden's premises in Handsworth. A garage and parking area was located on Alfred Road and adjoining offices on Soho Road.

Ken Flight's application to operate a daily service to London's Heathrow Airport had taken some time to secure, but the first services began in 1977 with one daily departure in each direction. The service began at the Alfred Road depot and picked-up at several Birmingham city centre hotels, Birmingham New Street station, Birmingham Airport and the National Exhibition Centre – the last pick-up was at the Hilton Hotel in Stratford Upon Avon. An arrangement with Air India enabled passengers to check-in for their flight at Flight's Coach Terminal prior to boarding the coach – on arrival at Heathrow passenger's luggage was loaded directly on to the aircraft. These early services would form the start of the Flightlink operation that would play an important part in the future success of the company.

By 1980, four departures each day were offered to Heathrow with additional pick-up points available at Walsall, Wolverhampton and Dudley on some departures. The "Flightlink" branding was introduced in the early 1980's and service numbers to the timetable from "101" onwards. The route was eventually extended to serve Gatwick and, by 1984 Luton Airport was offered on certain departures followed by Manchester Airport.

Customer service and reliability was imperative to the successful operation of Flightlink and Flight's attention to detail ensured that the whole operation was comparable to the standards set by airlines. A computer system was installed to handle bookings from around 900 travel agents and British Airways offices worldwide. All coaches were equipped with on-board toilets, refreshment facilities and video systems. Each vehicle had a dedicated "coach captain" who was responsible for the vehicle and its crew – every departure had at least two drivers. All coaches had two-way radio systems which enabled constant contact with the traffic office which was manned 24-hours each day.

Double-deck coaches were introduced to the operation in 1985 when seven Jonckheere Jubilee P95 bodied Volvo B10MTs were acquired. These seated 67 passengers and had a huge 13.4 cubic metres of luggage space which, enabled passengers' baggage for different airports to be stored separately – resulting in faster loading and unloading. British coach builder Plaxton, developed their Paramount range to include a similar design known as the Paramount 4000RS – Flight's took delivery of four in 1986 on Volvo chassis and this combination became the standard vehicle for Flightlink operations with 19 examples purchased between 1986 and 1990.

As the number of Flightlink departures increased, high specification single-deck coaches replaced twin deck vehicles on most journeys. Fourteen DAF powered Bova Futura integrals were purchased during 1994 and 1995 which, together with three double-deck Neoplan Skyliners new in 1995, formed the Flightlink fleet of that period. These vehicles were painted in a revised version of the fleet colours in cream with black lower skirt panels that had four narrow silver stripes and one broader red stripe and new "Flightlink" fleet name. The revised livery was adopted for all new fleet purchases – Flightlink vehicles had the strap line "Your Passport to the Airport", whilst other vehicles had "People to places in style" alongside the Flight's name.

Although it took a number of years to build up, the Flightlink range of services was hugely successful – its growth had mirrored the expansion of air-travel. At its peak around 400,000 passengers were carried annually, and the vehicles used on the services covered between 80,000 and 100,000 miles each year. Plans were made to extend the range of services offered including departures from Nottingham and the East Midlands area, however, in a surprise move, the Flightlink brand and its services was sold to National Express in 1996 – Flight's, however continued to provide coaches on contract. National Express adopted the Flightlink name nationwide for most of its airport links and other contractor's vehicles received a simplified version of the Flightlink livery. This arrangement however ceased during one of National Express's numerous re-branding exercises, and the "National Express Airport" title adopted on white coaches.

Throughout the 1980's and early 1990's, Flightlink was perhaps the most highly visible of Flight's operations, but it was only one part of the company's activities. During the early 1980's coach holiday de-regulation enabled those who wanted to, to operate coach tours without the need to obtain a licence. For a short time holidays by express coach to the South of France and Spain were very popular, and cheaper, alternatives to air-travel. With a fleet of comfortable coaches, Flight's launched their "Super Sun" holidays programme offering a range of holidays options including hotels, self-catering apartments and mobile homes at the Mediterranean resorts of France and Spain.

Other holidays and short breaks were also offered and some day excursions including a series of "Dine in the Sky" trips. This innovative idea saw collaboration with British Airways when the Boeing 747 was first introduced into the BA fleet. Passengers were transferred to Heathrow by coach and then boarded a 747 for a 2-hour flight with dinner and champagne on board. British Airways used the flight for staff training and the trips were very popular. Similar excursions were later offered which included a flight on Concorde.

Five Plaxton Viewmaster bodied Volvo B58s were purchased in 1980 and were followed in 1982 by the first completely foreign vehicles in the shape of four MAN powered Van-Hool T8 Acron integral coaches. These arrived, and entered service, in time for a busy summer schedule on Flight's "Super Sun" holidays programme to the South of France and Spain. The following year saw five twin-deck Van-Hool Astrons acquired which had a downstairs lounge incorporating a kitchen area and, in 1986, a double-deck Setra S228DT became the fleet flagship. These vehicles offered a high degree of passenger comfort for the long-distance holiday transfers and were worked hard – often completing 2 round trips in a week clocking up over 4000 miles each week.

Pick-ups for these holidays were available from the Birmingham area as well Luton and London. A separate development saw a coach travel only option become available under the "Euro Flight" title. Although popular for a number of years, increased competition from non-coach operating tour operators and lower air-travel prices lead Flight's to leave this market place and concentrate on more lucrative business sectors.

Ken Flight's wife, Gwen, assisted in the running of the business, and their son Geoff also joined the family firm in 1979 – later becoming Managing Director. Daughter, Sheila Ann Wheeler, also joined the company and managed the Flight's Conference services division. The National Exhibition Centre, International Convention Centre and National Indoor Arena in Birmingham offered many opportunities in the Corporate and Exhibition sectors with local transfers and social programmes. Flights handled the transportation for many major events including the World Gymnastic championships, the World Figure Skating championships, Rover 600 launch, Land Rover Discovery launch, the Lions convention, the Ryder Cup and Rotary International Conference in 1994 – to name a but a few. The high standards of service offered by the company were recognised in 1989, when Flights won the English Tourist Board's "England for Excellence" Tourism Award.

Apart from the dedicated Flightlink vehicles, the coach fleet became almost standardised on

Operating a large, quality, coach fleet, placed Flights in an excellent position to handle transportation requirements for the many large conferences and events that took place at the NEC and the International Convention Centre in Birmingham. In this view coaches are lined for departure during the World Lions Convention at the NEC. *Ken Flight collection*

Plaxton bodied Volvo products, although a batch of Dennis Javelins with Plaxton Premiere 320 bodies was acquired in 1997. Other types operated include three Irizar bodied Scania tri-axles and the first 10-metre Bova Futura to be imported into the UK market. Other small vehicles operated included several Toyota – Caetano Optimos as well as two 9-metre Bedords with Plaxton Paramount bodies. A used Bristol LHS with completely re-furbished Plaxton Supreme body also saw service in the late 1980's mainly as a feeder vehicle.

In 1992 a bus service operated under the "Flightrider" title was started. This served Perry Barr and West Bromwich. Three Mercedes mini coaches with PMT bodies were used on the route.

By the early 1990's the company had outgrown the premises in Handsworth so a suitable new operating centre was sought. In 1994 a four and a half-acre site in Aston become available when Bristol Street Motors vacated their commercial depot at Long Acre. These premises offered an extensive maintenance garage, large parking area and first class offices. Flights refurbished all of the buildings and incorporated a dedicated Flightlink reception and departure bay. The enlarged facilities also enabled a new division, Flight's Motor Services, to be set-up. This offered commercial vehicle servicing and recovery services. Service agencies were held for Dennis and Unitec vehicles. When the refurbishment was completed, an open evening was held and the premises officially opened by the Deputy Lord Mayor of Birmingham.

In 1996 the company successfully bid to operate the car park shuttle service at the National Exhibition Centre when the contract was offered for renewal. Previously operated by high-floor coaches, the new contract called for a dedicated fleet of low-floor vehicles. Ten Plaxton Pointer bodied Dennis Darts were acquired and were painted in white livery with NEC logo and lettering.

Expansion in 1997 saw the Coaching Division of West Midlands Travel being acquired. This operated under the "Central Liner" title and had evolved following the West Midland Travel take-over of Walsall based Central Coachways. Central Liner had operated a wide range of coaching activities including private hire, holidays and excursions and a daily service to London – this originally commenced as a joint venture with London Coaches. Apart from private hire, most of these services had ceased by the time Flights bought the operation. Seventeen coaches – a mix of Bova Futuras and Van-Hool bodied DAFs and some Ikarus bodied-Volvo B10Ms were acquired but were soon disposed of. The acquisition also bought with it the contract to supply the team coach for Aston Villa – a welcome return to Flight's operations after a short absence.

During the late 1990's a separate company, "Advantage Chauffeur Services" was established, which offered a fleet of chauffeur driven Jaguar and BMW saloons, as well as people carriers, to the Business and Corporate sector. This operation was very successful and grew to around 20 vehicles. A brief period of operating coach holidays also took

Left to right: The Deputy Lord Mayor of Birmingham, Geoff Flight and Ken Flight at the official opening of Flight's new Headquarters at Long Acre in 1994. *Ken Flight collection*

place within The Flights Travel Group at around this time. Unfortunately the coach holiday market in general suffered a downturn as a combined result of increased competition from low-cost air travel and the foot and mouth epidemic and that part of the group was disposed of in 2001.

The new millennium saw a stunning Neoplan Starliner acquired as fleet flagship and the latest coach to transport the Aston Villa team. With 1 FTO registration, this coach was entered in the 2001 UK Coach Rally and earned Flight's 6th "Coach of the Year" title – an achievement unequalled by any other operator to date.

A heritage coach fleet was established with the purchase of two former fleet members. The first acquired was 1960 Harrington Cavalier bodied AEC Reliance, 477 AOP. This was followed by 1953 Burlingham Seagull bodied AEC Regal, TOB 377 – which was one of Ken Flight's personal favourites. Both vehicles were completely stripped down and re-built to "as new" condition and were available to hire for special events.

Ken Flight had been involved in the family business since the 1940's and built up the company to become one of the most well known and respected within the coach travel industry. Flight's had an enviable reputation which was built through first class customer service, attention to detail and an exceptional level of presentation throughout the whole company. Upon Ken's retirement in 2002, the Birmingham based fleet was sold to Nottingham based Dunn Line. The Flights brand continued as a separate unit within the Dunn Line group until sold by them in October 2004 to Centra – a bus operating division of Central Parking Systems, which also owned Hallmark Coaches. Centra amalgamated the two companies to form "Flights Hallmark". This period of ownership was however short lived and, after a complicated series of events, the combined Flights-Hallmark operation was acquired by Rotala plc in 2005.

Following the acquisition of Flights Hallmark, a number of small bus operators have been acquired including Birmingham Motor Traction, Zaks Buses and North Birmingham Busways. The largest acquisition took place in 2008 when Diamond Bus was acquired from the Go Ahead group. A further purchase in 2008 saw family owned Ludlows being acquired.

Today, Rotala has developed into a company operating around 520 vehicles from centres in Birmingham, Bristol, London Gatwick, London Heathrow, Redditch and Tividale. The current Group operations comprise…

Diamond Bus Company
This company operates buses from two operating centres – the main depot being the former Birmingham Coach Company / Diamond Buses premises in Tividale, which now also incorporates the former Ludlows fleet. This depot runs buses in the Black Country under the "Black Diamond" name. A second depot is located at Redditch, which operates as "Red Diamond". September 2009 saw further expansion of this operation, with an additional depot opened, and a network of services commenced, in Worcester.

Flights Hallmark
This is the coach operating division of the group working from the group's head office in Birmingham and from depots at Gatwick and Heathrow. The vehicles are employed on Air crew contracts, Corporate contracts and hire, as well as providing VIP coaches for premiership football teams including, of course, Aston Villa. The Birmingham operation handled all of the ground transport requirements for the 100th Rotary International Conference held staged in Birmingham in June 2009.

Central Connect
Operating from Long Acre in Birmingham, this fleet is employed on contract, and some commercial routes in Birmingham. The operation has evolved from the amalgamation of the former Zaks, North Birmingham Busways and Birmingham Motor Traction fleets. The latest vehicles for this fleet operate under the Signature brand in Solihull.

Wessex Connect
Wessex Connect operates vehicles in the Bristol area from a depot at Filton. A number of contracted services for Bristol Council, South Gloucestershire Council, Bath and North Somerset Council and the University of the West of England are operated by this division.

Thus, in the 21st century, nearly 100 years since Frank Flight started his taxi and garage business, the Flight name continues within the Rotala Group. The Flight family connection continues, as Geoff Flight is a Director and shareholder of Rotala plc, which is listed on the Alternative Investment Market. The group now has a turnover of over £40,000,000 per annum and has become a major provider of contracted and commercial bus and coach operations throughout the country.

A Pictorial History of Flights Coaches

1997 – Flights recommence coach operating with five Leyland Leopards fitted with high-floor Plaxton Viewmaster bodies. A clause in the sale in 1973 to L F Bowen prevented the Flight name being used until 1979. Until then, the fleet name of Forward Coaches was used – "Forward" being taken from the City of Birmingham motto and coat of arms. All five Viewmasters are pictured here at the former Sugden's Coaches depot on Alfred Road in Handsworth. *Pete Southern collection*

The "Forward" fleet name is displayed on ROE 701R – note the "Express" type doors and the additional bright mouldings and marker lights specified. All coaches were delivered in 1977, the first three in June: ROE 700/701 and 703R and the last two in August: SOJ 702 and 704S. *Colin Ludford*

85

DAILY SERVICES by FORWARD Coaches Birmingham Ltd

NEC DIRECT COACH LINK

- NATIONAL EXHIBITION CENTRE
- LONDON HEATHROW AIRPORT
- BIRMINGHAM AREA HOTELS & AIRPORT
- STRATFORD UPON-AVON HOTELS

Fares & Time Table

A licence was obtained to operate a daily service connecting Birmingham and Stratford upon Avon hotels to Birmingham Airport, the National Exhibition Centre and Heathrow Airport. This service formed the basis of "Flightlink" which would be an important part of the future success of Flight's Coach Travel.

The Motor Show at the NEC in 1978 presented an excellent opportunity for the service. Special leaflets were produced and distributed. The £1.00 return fare is excellent value when the high parking charges imposed by the NEC are considered.

MOTOR SHOW
DESTINATION NEC and LONDON HEATHROW
16th-29th OCTOBER 1978
OUTWARD SERVICE
BIRMINGHAM HOTELS-NEC-LONDON HEATHROW

HOTELS	Depart	Depart	Depart	Fares to and from NEC	Fares to and from Heathrow
FORWARD COACH STATION & CAR PARK	06.00	07.30		£1.00	
'POST HOUSE', GREAT BARR	06.20	07.45	10.30	£1.00	£6.90
'EUROPA LODGE', WEST BROMWICH	06.30	07.55	10.40	£1.00	£6.80
'LAMBERT COURT', HAGLEY ROAD	06.43	08.06	10.51	£1.00	£6.80
'PLAZA', HAGLEY ROAD	06.45	08.10	10.55	£1.00	£6.80
'EATON', HAGLEY ROAD	06.46	08.12	10.57	£1.00	£6.80
'NORFOLK', HAGLEY ROAD	06.47	08.16	11.01	£1.00	£6.80
'APOLLO', HAGLEY ROAD	06.49	08.18	11.03	£1.00	£6.80
'STRATHALLAN' & 'COBDEN', HAGLEY ROAD	06.49	08.22	11.07	£1.00	£6.80
'PLOUGH & HARROW', HAGLEY ROAD	06.52	08.25	11.10	£1.00	£6.80
'HOLIDAY INN', SUFFOLK STREET	07.01	08.35	11.20	£1.00	£6.70
'ALBANY', SMALLBROOK RINGWAY	07.03	08.40	11.25	£1.00	£6.70
'GRAND', COLMORE ROW	07.05	08.45	11.30	£1.00	£6.70
'ROYAL ANGUS', ST. CHADS QUEENSWAY	07.07	08.50	11.35	£1.00	£6.70
'METROPOLE'	07.25	09.13		.07p	
NEC WEST COACH PARK ARRIVE	07.30	09.15	12.00		
NOTE: Fully loaded coaches, booked in advance, will go DIRECT to NEC from certain HOTELS.					
NEC WEST COACH PARK DEPART	07.32	09.17		.07p	£6.10
'METROPOLE'	07.33	09.18			£6.10
BIRMINGHAM AIRPORT	07.50	09.35		.10p	£6.00
'HILTON', STRATFORD-UPON-AVON	08.22	10.07			£5.00
LONDON HEATHROW AIRPORT:— SETTING DOWN AT TERMINALS AND CENTRAL BUS/TUBE STATION	10.10	12.00			

*THIS TIMING DOES NOT OPERATE ON 16th, 17th, 18th, 19th OCTOBER.

BOOK SEATS at HOTELS TRAVEL BUREAUS or on COACHES when boarding
ALL FARES ARE FOR SINGLE JOURNEYS   RETURN TIMES overleaf

A GREAT SERVICE TO MEET THE TRANSPORTATION NEEDS OF A GREAT SHOW.

FORWARD Coaches Birmingham Ltd
4 Alfred Road, Handsworth, Birmingham B21 9LY England.
Phone: Chart Room 021-523 4141 or 021-551 4189   Telex: 336512

Leyland Leopard, ROE 700R is pictured at the NEC during the period of the Motor Show with special boards fitted to the side panels. *PM Photography*

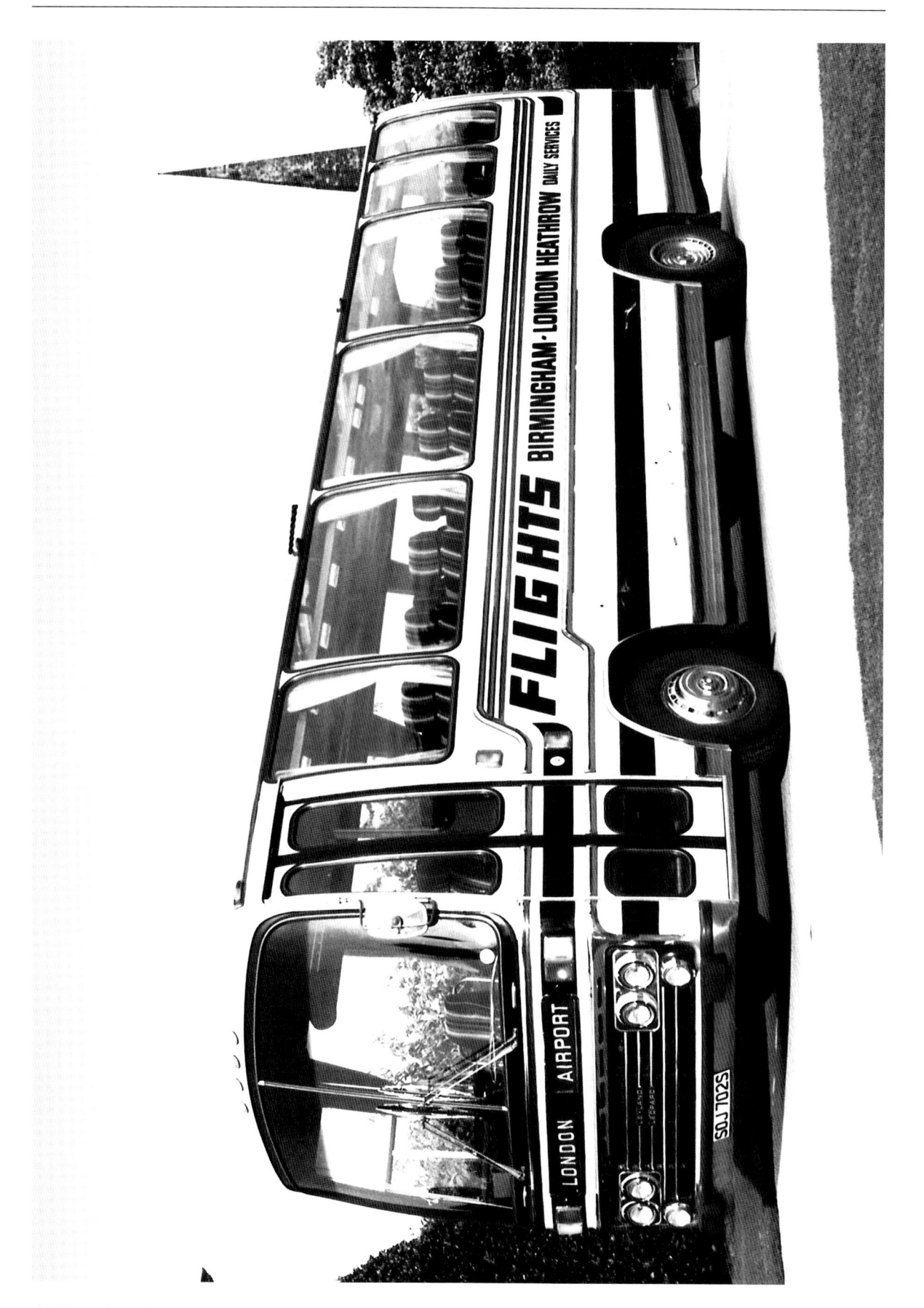

1979 – The Flight name is restored to coaching as the "Flights Coach Travel" replaces the Forward Coaches identity. Plaxton Viewmaster bodied Leyland Leopard; SOJ 702S is pictured in the grounds of Aston Hall and displays the new fleet name. *Ken Flight collection*

SOJ 704S pictured at the Alfred Road premises. Discreet runners were fitted between the stainless steel trim on these vehicles to enable boards for the Heathrow service to be displayed when required. *Colin Ludford*

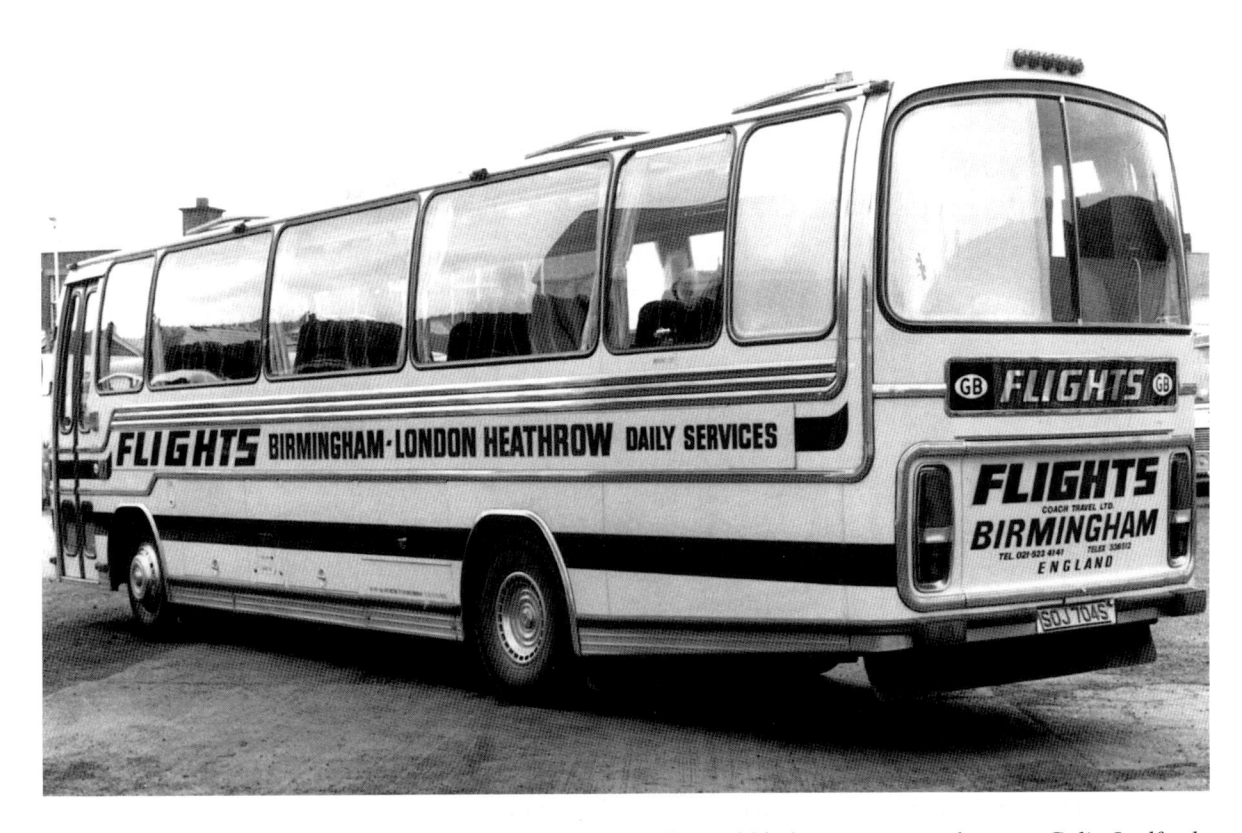

A rear view of SOJ 704S – this coach was fitted with a toilet and kitchen servery at the rear. *Colin Ludford*

A Pictorial History of Flights Coaches

The facility to have boards with their name or message was made available to corporate clients – as seen here on SOJ 704S whilst working for the Pirelli tyre company. *PM Photography*

A general shortage of good drivers creates problems for coach operators in the 21st century – however there was probably no shortage of volunteers for this journey in the late 1970's. Contestants for the Miss World title pose for the camera before boarding their Flight's Coach at the Strathallan Hotel in Birmingham – the driver is John Thompson. *Ken Flight collection*

Flights – People to Places in Style

London Heathrow service timetable – circa 1979. An arrangement was made with Air India for passengers to check in for their flight at Flight's depot.

FLIGHTS COACH TRAVEL LTD
TO LONDON HEATHROW AIRPORT
DAILY SERVICES from £5.00 by SUPER LUXURY COACHES

FLIGHTS COACH TRAVEL LTD
TO BIRMINGHAM
The National Exhibition Centre
The West Midlands Area
Stratford upon Avon
DAILY SERVICES from £5.00 by SUPER LUXURY COACHES

FLIGHTS COACH TRAVEL LTD
NON-STOP EXPRESS DAILY to and from LONDON Heathrow

OUTWARD to LONDON	Fare £5.00
Departing BIRMINGHAM FLIGHTS Coach Air Terminal 294-296 SOHO ROAD, HANDSWORTH	06.00 hrs.
Arriving LONDON Heathrow Terminals	08.30 hrs.
RETURN to BIRMINGHAM	Fare £5.00
Departing LONDON Heathrow From Central Bus Station Loading Bay U The Bus Station is connected by moving pathways with baggage facilities from all terminals.	10.45 hrs.
Arriving BIRMINGHAM FLIGHTS Coach Air Terminal 294-296 SOHO ROAD, HANDSWORTH	13.15 hrs.

For friends and relatives seeing off or meeting Passengers:
Special Same Day Return Fare only £5.00 Return

CHILDREN aged 2-12 years 50% off above fares

AIR-INDIA
SPECIAL CHECK-IN AND BAGGAGE WEIGHING SERVICE AT OUR COACH STATION
Avoid queueing and waiting at Heathrow terminal.

FLIGHTS COACH TRAVEL LTD
WEST MIDLANDS SERVICE and NATIONAL EXHIBITION CENTRE to and from LONDON Heathrow

Symbols	PICK-UP POINTS and TIME TABLE	READ DOWN		READ UP		Fares to or from Heathrow	Fares to or from NEC
X ↔ □ P	FLIGHTS COACH-AIR TERMINAL, BIRMINGHAM	Depart	07.40	Arrive	18.20	£6.90	£1.00
X ↔ □ P	POST HOUSE HOTEL, GREAT BARR, WALSALL RD.	"	08.00	"	18.00	£6.90	£1.00
X ↔ □ P	EUROPA LODGE HOTEL, WEST BROMWICH	"	08.10	"	17.50	£6.80	£1.00
X	LAMBERT COURT, HAGLEY ROAD, BIRMINGHAM	"	08.23	"	17.37	£6.80	£1.00
	PLAZA HOTEL, HAGLEY ROAD	"	08.25	"	17.35	£6.80	£1.00
P	NORFOLK HOTEL, HAGLEY ROAD	"	08.27	"	17.33	£6.80	£1.00
X ↔ □ P	STRATHALLEN HOTEL, HAGLEY RD	"	08.29	"	17.31	£6.80	£1.00
P	PLOUGH & HARROW HOTEL, HAGLEY RD	"	08.32	"	17.28	£6.80	£1.00
X ↔ □ P	HOLIDAY INN HOTEL, CITY CENTRE, BIRMINGHAM	"	08.41	"	17.19	£6.70	£1.00
P	ALBANY HOTEL, SMALLBROOK RINGWAY	"	—	"	17.16	£6.70	
X ↔ □	BRITISH RAIL, NEW STREET STATION FORECOURT	"	08.45	"	17.15	£6.70	
	METROPOLE HOTEL & CONFERENCE CENTRE	"	09.05	"	16.55	£6.10	.07p
X ↔ □	NATIONAL EXHIBITION CENTRE PIAZZA	"	09.10	"	16.50	£6.10	
X ↔ □	BIRMINGHAM AIRPORT DEPARTURE BUILDING	"	09.30	"	16.30	£6.00	.10p
X ↔ □	STRATFORD-UPON-AVON, opp. HILTON HOTEL	"	10.02	"	15.58	£5.00	
	ARRIVING LONDON HEATHROW AIRPORT,			LONDON HEATHROW			To or From NEC or Birmingham Airport
□ P	TERMINAL BUILDING No. 1	Arrive	12.00	Departing 14.00 hrs from:			
□ P	" " No. 2	"	12.05	London Heathrow Airport,			
X ↔ □ P	" " No. 3	"	12.10	Bay U, Central Bus Station.			
X ↔ □	HEATHROW CENTRAL BUS/STATION	"	12.12				
↔ □	HEATHROW HOTEL MAIN ENTRANCE	"	12.17	READ UP			

SYMBOLS DENOTE:
- X CONSOLIDATION POINTS for other passengers staying in area.
- ↔ FULLY LOADED COACH will proceed direct.
- □ TAXI STANDS OR POINTS AVAILABLE
- P CAR PARKING AVAILABLE short or long term.

During all CONFERENCES & EXHIBITIONS local daily services

90

A Pictorial History of Flights Coaches

1979 – Two Leyland Leopards with Plaxton Supreme IV bodies were purchased this year. COF 705V was the first registered and is pictured here at the Handsworth garage. *Colin Ludford*

COF 707V was the second of the pair – note that the stainless steel trim has again been modified to suit the position of the fleet name and to accommodate the runners for Flight's name boards (not fitted in this view). *Colin Ludford*

Both coaches had the "Express" version of Plaxton's Supreme body with twin passenger entrance doors – evident in this view of COF 705V photographed at Pool Meadow, Coventry. *Andrew Roberts*

Flights – People to Places in Style

1980 – Five 12-metre Volvo B58s with Plaxton Viewmaster IV bodies joined the fleet this year. GOP 710W demonstrates the revised livery applied to these coaches incorporating an upswept black and silver stripe.
Ken Flight collection

An interior view of one of the batch with tables fitted and a rear servery and toilet. The seats were of Plaxton's "relaxa 2" design and were just one of the many extra items specified on these vehicles.
Ken Flight collection

A Pictorial History of Flights Coaches

GOP 708W is pictured on the French Riviera after dropping off passengers at one of Flight's "Supersun" destinations. *Ken Flight collection*

Another Plaxton bodied Volvo – GOP 730W is pictured whilst working a Flightlink service. It was not uncommon for these vehicles to operate 2 round trips between Birmingham and Gatwick each day. *PM Photography*

Flights – People to Places in Style

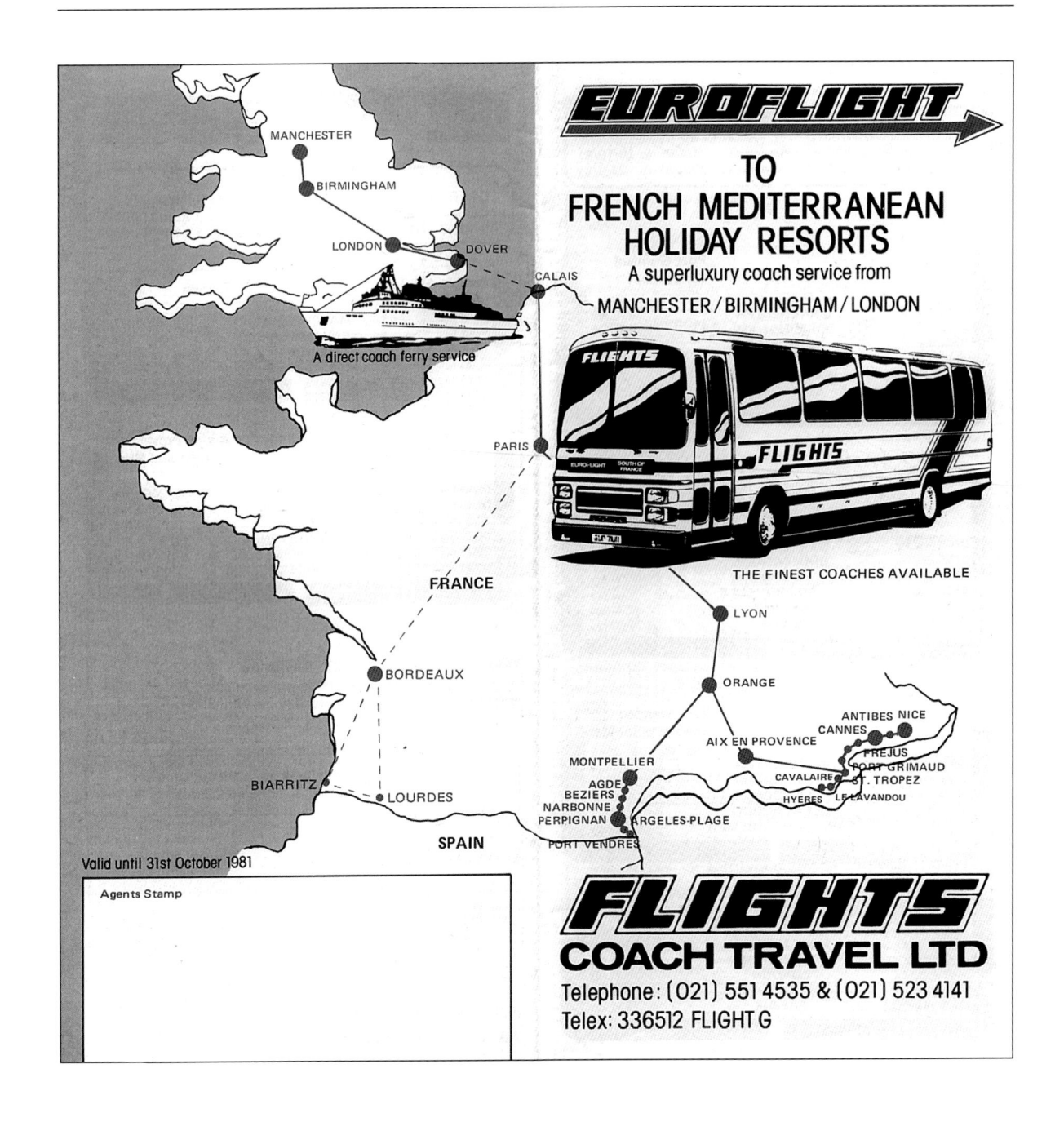

Operated in conjunction with the "Supersun" holidays programme, "Euroflight" services made available a coach travel only option to passengers wishing to travel to the French Riviera resorts. Departures were available from Birmingham, London and Manchester.

1982 – The first fully continental built coaches join the fleet with four integral Van-Hool T8 Acrons. With MAN engines, these vehicles were fitted with 49 reclining seats, toilet /washroom, and video system and regularly clocked up 4000 miles each week when operating 2 round trips to the South of France and Spanish holiday resorts. NOX 740X, NOX 750X, NOX 770X and NOX 777X are pictured at the Birmingham Flightlink terminal. *Ken Flight collection*

Two of the Van-Hool Acrons were entered in the 28th British Coach Rally at Brighton – Flight's first entrants since 1972. NOX 770X is pictured en-route to Brighton with Roger Ludlow driving.
Ken Flight collection

Geoff Flight drove the second entry, NOX 777X, which is seen here on Madeira Drive. The livery was modified on these coaches and a new "Flights Travel Group" logo adopted. *Andrew Roberts collection*

A rear view of NOX 777X on Madeira Drive – note the "Euro Flight Express" board on the engine cover door and the destinations covered by Flights Supersun Holidays. The panel was changed when vehicles were operated on Flightlink services. *Ken Flight collection*

The Flight's team at the 1982 coach rally – left to right: Paul Kennedy, Philippe Shufflebotham, Roger Ludlow, John Thompson, Sheila Wheeler, Geoff Flight. NOX 707X was awarded the trophy for "Best coach in Class". *Ken Flight collection*

Flights – People to Places in Style

To cope with additional demand four Leyland Leopards were leased for the 1982 season from Arlington Motor Company. Two had Plaxton Supreme IV bodies – as represented here by DBH 451X pictured at Pool Meadow in Coventry whilst working a Flightlink duty. *Daniel Hill collection*

The other two coaches had Duple Dominant III bodies including DBH 453X seen here. The Dominant III featured small double glazed slanted windows – the design developed for the Scottish Bus Group's motorway fleet. These four coaches remained with Flights for around nine months. *PM Photography*

1983 – Five integral Van-Hool T818 Astron coaches were added to the fleet this year. These vehicles seated 60 passengers – 50 in the main saloon on the upper deck and ten in a lounge behind the rear axle which incorporated a kitchen area. Each coach had a 280 BHP MAN engine and ZF automatic gearbox. One of the five is pictured prior to delivery. *Andrew Roberts collection*

Flights – People to Places in Style

Van-Hool Astron, TOA 737Y is pictured whilst advertising Flight's "Supersun" holiday programme. The main passenger entrance was located behind the rear axle on these coaches. *Daniel Hill photography*

TOA 747Y is seen here at the Moet & Chandon Chateau in Epernay, France. Extra large fuel tanks fitted to these vehicles allowed an operational range of more than 1000 miles. *Ken Flight collection*

A Pictorial History of Flights Coaches

1984 "Supersun" holidays brochure. This featured holidays to the French Riviera and Spanish resorts with accommodation options available that included hotels and mobile homes.

A great deal of effort was made to advertise the comfort and facilities of the coaches used for these journeys. Unlike many companies that offered this type of holiday, Flights operated their own vehicles and could guarantee the quality and standard of coaches provided.

Van-Hool Acrons and Astons pictured at the Handsworth depot preparing for another departure to the Mediterranean resorts. *Ken Flight collection*

Flights – People to Places in Style

1985 – B703 EOF, one of five Scania K112 chassis with Jonckheere Jubilee P599 49-seat bodies purchased this year. The P599 was a variant of the Jonckheere P50 body with a lowered driving position and deep two-piece windscreen – a popular feature on many coaches of the 1980's. *PM Photography*

An offside view of the first of the batch B700 EOF – note that the "Flightlink" name is displayed rather than the normal Flights lettering. Airport destinations are applied to the tops of the side windows. *Andrew Roberts collection*

Seven other Jonckheere bodied coaches also joined the fleet in 1985 – all were of the Jubilee P95 model with 67-seats and built on Volvo B10MT chassis. These coaches had a huge locker space of 13.4 cubic metres, which enabled passengers' luggage for different airports to be loaded in separate sections when operating on Flightlink services. Five of the seven are pictured at the Belfry Hotel, Sutton Coldfield.
Ken Flight collection

Flights – People to Places in Style

Ken Flight receiving the keys for the new coaches from Bill Russell of Volvo with Chris Verbaceys from Jonckheere (left) and Tony Harvy of Volvo (right). *Ken Flight collection*

Ken Flight pictured with the coach captains and hostesses. Left to right: Lee Allen, John Wood, Jane Insley, Ken Flight, Eva, Dave Sinclair, Jackie Rabbitt, Roy Berry and Mick Howell. *Ken Flight collection*

Jonckheere P95 bodied Volvo, B707 EOF is seen at Heathrow Airport whilst operating a Flightlink service. *PM Photography*

Another of the batch, B708 EOF is pictured in Birmingham passing St.Martins Church and the old Bull Ring Market. *Daniel Hill collection*

The last of the Volvo – Jonckheere P95s was delivered in August 1985 and thus received a C pre-fix registration – C712 GOP. *Andrew Roberts collection*

To compete with similar continental designs, Plaxton developed their Paramount range to include a twin deck variant – the 4000RS. Flights purchased 4 in 1986 including C720 GOP, which was exhibited by Plaxton at the British Coach Rally. *PM Photography*

A Pictorial History of Flights Coaches

1973 brochure for Continental coach cruises and Express services.

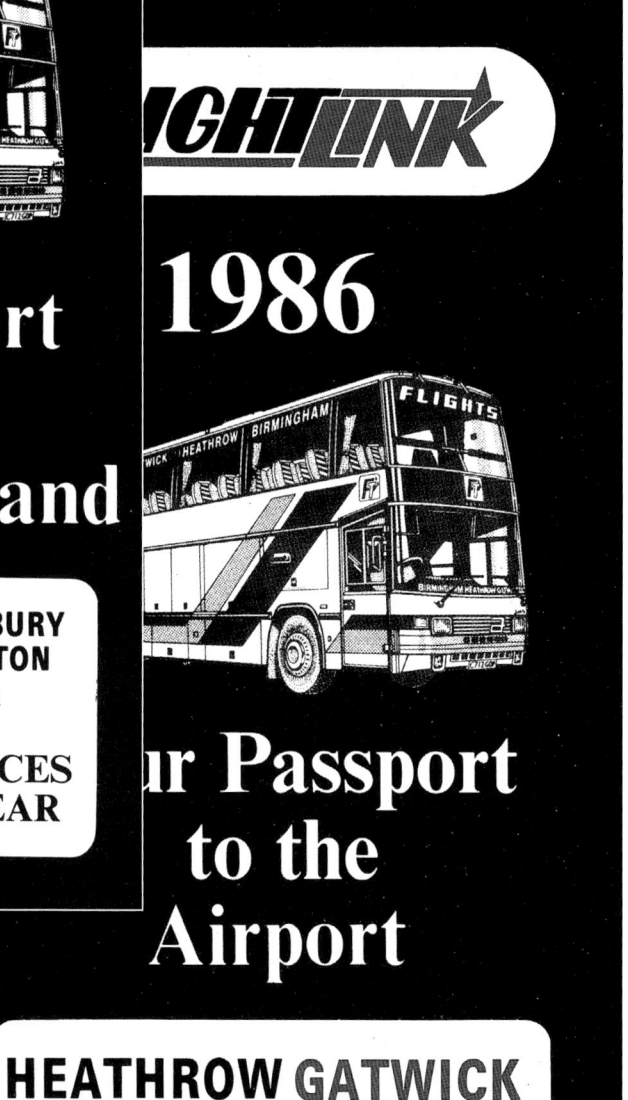

FLIGHTLINK

1986

Your Passport to the Heart of England

HIGH WYCOMBE OXFORD BANBURY
WARWICK LUTON NORTHAMPTON
COVENTRY BIRMINGHAM &
WOLVERHAMPTON
LUXURY COACH SERVICES
THROUGHOUT THE YEAR

FLIGHTLINK

1986

Your Passport to the Airport

HEATHROW GATWICK
LUTON BIRMINGHAM
LUXURY COACH SERVICES
THROUGHOUT THE YEAR

107

Flights – People to Places in Style

1986 – C770 GOP, a Kassbohrer Setra S228DT 74-seater. This was the only Setra to be operated by the company. *Ken Flight collection*

Although this coach saw duty on a variety of operations, it was purchased mainly for the long distance shuttles of Flight's Supersun Holidays. The livery was modified to suit the double-deck design and the fleet name was originally applied in red rather than black. *Ken Flight collection*

A Pictorial History of Flights Coaches

C770 GOP was entered in the 1986 British Coach Rally and claimed another "Coach of the Year" title for Flights. The coach is pictured on Madeira Drive following completion of the Saturday driving test. *Andrew Roberts*

The winning team – driver Lee Allen and hostess Maxine Leighton with C770 GOP and the "Coach of the Year" trophy. *Ken Flight collection*

Flights – People to Places in Style

1987 – Virtually all coaches were acquired brand new, however a small number of used vehicles were also purchased. One such vehicle was FTG 5, a 1983 Volvo B10M with a Duple Caribbean body to full executive 36-seat specification. *Daniel Hill photography*

1988 – Two more Plaxton Paramount 4000RS bodied Volvo B10MT chassis were acquired this year. One of the pair, E777 VDA is pictured here. *Daniel Hill photography*

Five further Plaxton bodied Volvos were also purchased in 1988 – all B10M chassis with Paramount 3500 III LS bodies. E577 VDA is pictured here outside the Flightlink terminal in Handsworth. *Daniel Hill photography*

Another of the batch, E277 VJW – the fleet name of these coaches was modified and this style would become standard for all future new purchases. *Daniel Hill photography*

Flights – People to Places in Style

1989 – Ten Volvo B10MT chassis with Plaxton Paramount 4000RS bodies were delivered between April and June this year including F702 COA. *Ken Flight collection*

F710 COA – another of the 1989 Plaxton 4000RS bodied Volvos – although used mainly on Flightlink services, the high seating capacity also made these vehicles popular for private hire groups. *PM photography*

A Pictorial History of Flights Coaches

FTG 9, one of two Plaxton bodied Bedford YMPs acquired in 1990. This coach was originally registered D602 TMR and was new to Bell's of Winterslow in 1987. The seating was reduced to accommodate a rear toilet / washroom making an ideal vehicle for private hire and feeders. *Andrew Roberts collection*

A line-up of Plaxton Paramount 4000RS bodied Volvo B10MTs at the Handsworth depot. Left to right: F702 COA, F703 COA, F704 COA, E677 VDA and C750 GOP. Full use of the rear panel was made to promote Flightlink Airport services. *Ken Flight collection*

1989 – Flights were voted winners in the transportation section in the "England for Excellence" awards sponsored by the English Tourist Board. Former British Airways chairman, Lord King, hands the award to Geoff Flight. *Ken Flight collection*

Full use was made of the award logo on vehicles and publicity material.

On April 2nd 1990, a new coach service was started between Wolverhampton, Birmingham and central London. Branded as "Flightlink Royale" this was a high quality service and offered set-down points on Baker Street, Park Lane and at Victoria Coach Station. Hotel breaks and theatre tickets were also available in conjunction with the service. Five departures to London each day were available, and six from the capital back to the Midlands – including a 23.45 departure aimed at Theatregoers. Unfortunately the route was short lived owing to intense competition from National Express.

1990 – Three more Volvo B10MTs with Plaxton Paramount 4000RS bodies were purchased. Geoff Flight (right) is pictured with Plaxton's representative with two of the three prior to delivery, at the body builder's Scarborough factory. *Andrew Roberts collection*

G717 JOG, one of the 1990 Volvo B10MTs pictured whilst operating a private hire duty. Between 1986 and 1990, Flights purchased 19 of these vehicles – the largest fleet of the type in the country. *Ken Flight collection*

Flights – People to Places in Style

Flights Conference Services was a separate division headed-up by Ken Flight's daughter, Sheila Ann Wheeler. Although based at the company's head office, a separate sales office was also operated within the International Convention Centre in central Birmingham.

The National Exhibition Centre and International Convention Centre created many opportunities for Corporate and Exhibition ground transport business. Being able to provide a large fleet of quality vehicles and experienced staff lead Flight's to handle many high profile events.

A Complete Package of Co-Ordination and Logistical Support for Conference and Event Organisers

1991 – H2 FTG, a Toyota Coaster chassis with Caetano Optimo II 18-seat body – one of two delivered this year. Following these vehicles, most new coaches received "FTG" registrations. *Andrew Roberts collection*

1992 – The Caetano Optimos delivered the previous year proved successful in operation so two further examples were purchased this year including J4 FTG. These two differed by having 21-seats fitted – note also the modification to the livery when compared to H2 FTG. *Ken Flight collection*

Flights – People to Places in Style

A surprise development in 1992 was the commencement of a bus service serving Perry Barr, Great Barr and West Bromwich. Three Mercedes-Benz 811D chassis with PMT Ami 35-seat bodies were acquired for the route. J8 FTG is pictured here shortly after delivery. *Ken Flight collection*

Built by the Engineering department of the former Potteris Motor Traction Company, these little buses operated under the "Flightrider" name. With coach seats, tinted windows and curtains, they offered passengers a high level of comfort. *Ken Flight collection*

J7 FTG is pictured in West Bromwich bus station whilst on service. *Andrew Roberts collection*

118

A Pictorial History of Flights Coaches

1990's coach charter brochure.

1993 – K20 FTG, a Volvo B10M with Plaxton Excalibur body – one of eight identical coaches delivered between December 1992 and March 1993. *Ken Flight collection*

K12 FTG and K14 FTG – all of these coaches were air-conditioned and seated 49 passengers and replaced the Plaxton Paramount bodied Volvo B10Ms of 1988. *Ken Flight collection*

A Pictorial History of Flights Coaches

Plaxton Excalibur bodied Volvo, K12 FTG, pictured at Birmingham Airport – this rear view shows the curved rear window and the parallel opening boot door of the original Excalibur and Premiere body – both of these features were replaced by Plaxton on later models. *Ken Flight collection*

K15 FTG and K20 FTG – the Excalibur body featured a "swept back" frontal design – clearly visible in this view. *Ken Flight collection*

Flights – People to Places in Style

During 1993, Flights once again started to regularly supply a coach to transport the Aston Villa football team to away matches. This high specification Bova Futura was acquired from Central Coachways and fully refurbished and allocated registration 1 FTO. *Ken Flight collection*

Front and rear views of 1 FTO. New to Central Coachways in 1989 as F907 CJW, this coach had just 25 leather-covered seats, washroom, galley kitchen etc. *Ken Flight collection*

A Pictorial History of Flights Coaches

1994 – The whole operation moved from Handsworth to a new base at Long Acre in Aston. The site was previously used by Bristol Street Motors for their commercial sales and service division, and offered extensive workshop facilities and parking for the coach fleet and a dedicated Flightlink departure lounge.

The offices and former showroom, known as Beacon House, were totally refurbished and created a high profile head office for the Flights Travel Group and reservations centre for Flightlink services.

A new division, Flights Motor Services, was set-up which undertook repairs and service work for other operators as well as providing recovery and emergency assistance. The garage to the right of this view was used to house the Advantage Chauffeur car fleet when that operation was started in the late 1990s. *All pictures Ken Flight collection.*

Flights – People to Places in Style

Brochure for Flights Motor Services – the new service and repair division established at the Long Acre Depot in Aston, Birmingham.

1994 – The Flightlink operation was revised this year with increased service departures. A new fleet of 8 well-appointed Bova Futura coaches replaced some of the double-deck vehicles operated on the services. One of the batch is pictured prior to entering service. *Ken Flight collection*

L11 FTG is pictured arriving back in Birmingham. These vehicles entered service in a new livery and "Flightlink" branding. *Daniel Hill photography*

1995 – six more integral Bova Futuras were purchased for Flightlink this year, including M30 FTG. *Andrew Roberts*

With the 1995 deliveries, a total of fourteen Bova Futuras were operated on Flightlink services. Twelve are lined up for the camera at Long Acre – this picture gives an idea of the extensive parking available at the site. *Ken Flight collection*

A Pictorial History of Flights Coaches

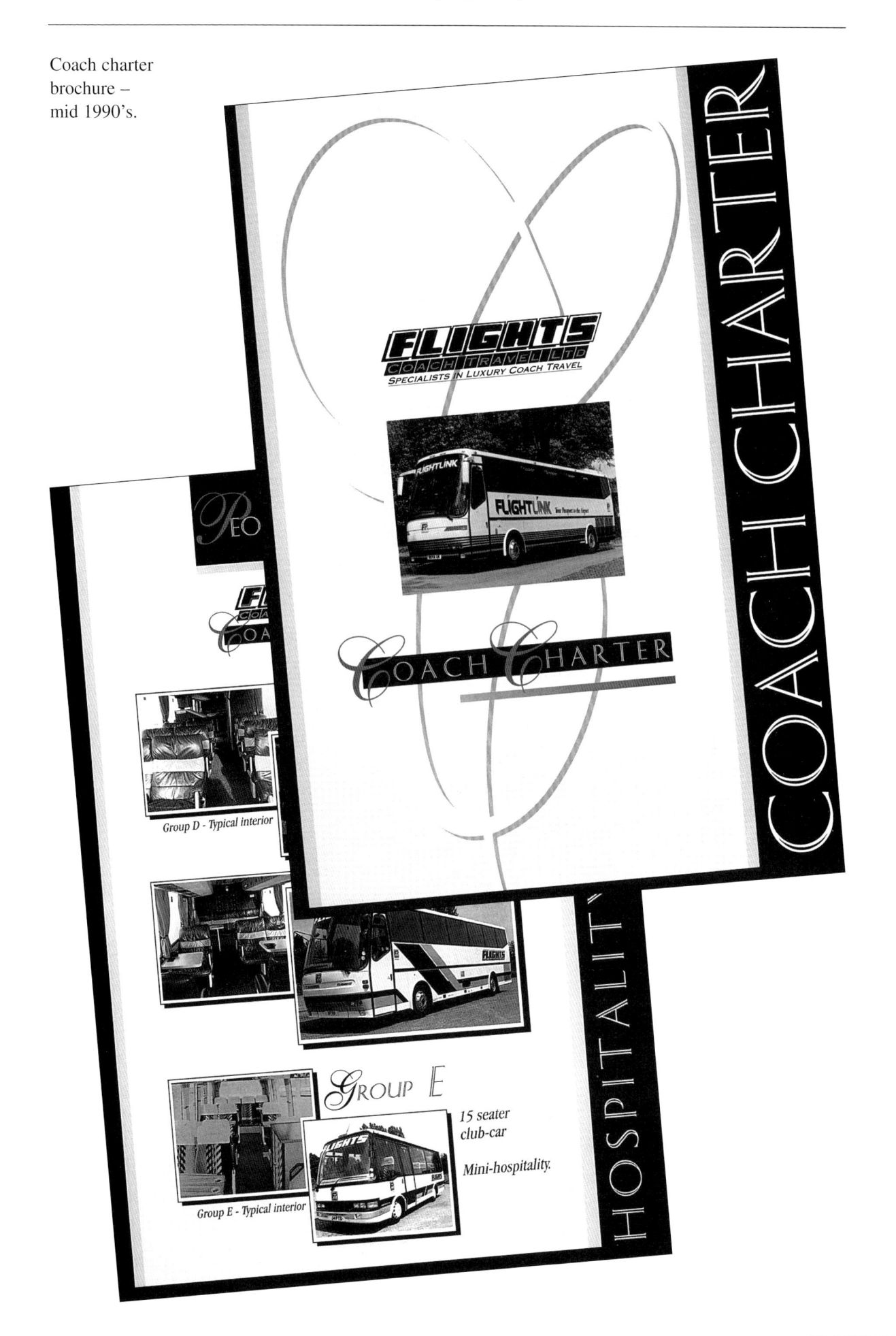

Coach charter brochure – mid 1990's.

127

Flights – People to Places in Style

Total Transport Management brochure – 1990s. As well as coach hire, Flights offered a complete logistical support service for conference and exhibition event organisers.

Total Transport Management from FLIGHTS COACH TRAVEL LTD

A Complete Package of Co-Ordination and Logistical Support for Conference, Exhibition and Event Organisers

A Winning Team

Flights Coach Travel are one of the most respected coach operators in Europe. We have our own fleet of super luxury coaches with a range of vehicles from 15 seater club cars to 61 seater twin decks, offering the flexibility to meet every demand and always ensuring the highest standards of safety, comfort and reliability.

Our dedicated Operations Team, with extensive local knowledge, is available to give maximum logistical support at the planning stages and come on board as part of your team to manage the transport requirements during the event. Uniformed, professional Drivers, drilled in the finer details of customer care and attention complement the operation.

Transfers Throughout Your Event.

*C*o-ordination

Throughout your event, we provide the staff to ensure a smooth, efficient operation of all ground transfer movements. With the benefit of our base-to-coach radio systems, our team of on-site traffic managers become an extension of your own staff, keeping abreast of any changes and informing you of any fine tuning requiremetnts to the satisfaction of you and your delegates.

A Pictorial History of Flights Coaches

Where To Find Us at The Airport

FLIGHTLINK *is well represented at the airports we serve. Below is listed details of where to find our offices or agents, what times they open and a telephone contact number.*

MANCHESTER
Terminal One– Tourist Information Desks
The FLIGHTLINK Desk is situated in the arrivals hall
Open: 0600 - 1100 hours
1300 - 2100 hours
Tel: 0161-489 8907
At all other times please contact the Tourist Information Desk
Open: 0800 - 2100 hours
Tel: 0161-436 3344

Terminal Two– Tourist Information Desk
Open: 0730 - 1230 hours
Tel: 0161-489 6412

HEATHROW
Terminals 1 & 2– Tickets and information can be obtained from the London Transport Desk.

Terminal 3– The FLIGHTLINK Office, is situated adjacent to the ARRIVALS COACH PARK. Open: 0630 - 2230 every day.
Tel: 0181-897 2596

Terminal 4– The FLIGHTLINK Agent is situated in the ARRIVALS HALL.
Open: 0600 - 2030 every day
Tel: 0181-745 4134

Central Bus Station– The FLIGHTLINK Agent is situated in the COACH TRAVEL CENTRE
Open: 0600 - 2100 every day
Tel: 0181-897 2596 or 0181-745 5445

GATWICK
North Terminal– The FLIGHTLINK Agent is situated at the Coach Information Desk in the ARRIVALS HALL.
Open: 0630 - 2130.
Tel: 01293-502359

South Terminal– The FLIGHTLINK Desk is situated in the ARRIVALS HALL.
Open: 0630 - 2100.
Tel: 01293-514244 or 01293-502177

BIRMINGHAM
Contact FLIGHTLINK Head Office– Beacon House, Long Acre, Birmingham
Fax: 0121-322 2240

FLIGHTLINK RECOMMEND YOU ARRIVE ONE HOUR BEFORE CHECK IN TIME.

FLIGHTLINK

Your Passport to the Airport

1995/96

LUXURY COACH TRAVEL

TO MANCHESTER, HEATHROW, GATWICK & BIRMINGHAM AIRPORTS

Valid From 14th April 1995

HEATHROW

FLIGHTLINK RECOMMEND YOU ARRIVE ONE HOUR BEFORE CHECK IN TIME.

BOARD AT THE FLIGHTLINK SIGN.

TO HEATHROW AIRPORT	CODE	101	102	104	105	106	107	108	109	110	111
WOLVERHAMPTON Bus Station, Pipers Row Express Coach Bay	WOL	0105	0220	0350	0450	0550	0650	0740	0950	1150	1350
HANDSWORTH Soho Road, Pump Tavern Bus Lay-By	SOH	0125	0240	0410	0510	0610	0710	0805	1010	1210	1410
BIRMINGHAM Smallbrook Ringway (Rotunda Lay-By)	ROT	0135	0250	0420	0520	0620	0720	0815	1020	1220	1420
FLIGHTLINK PASSENGER TERMINAL Long Acre, Aston. See Page 7	LAC	0145	0300	0430	0530	0630	0730	0830	1030	1230	1430
BIRMINGHAM AIRPORT Main Terminal Bus Stop	BHX	0200	0320	0450	0550	0650	0755	0855	1050	1250	1450
COVENTRY Pool Meadow Bus Station Stand Pd	CPM	0215	0340	0515	0615	0725	0830	0930	1125	1325	1525
WARWICK Outside Little Chef Southbound A46 Warwick By-Pass	WAR	0230	0400	0530	0630	0745	0850	0950	1145	1345	1545
BANBURY Bus Station Bay 7	BAN	0300	0430	0600	0700	0815	0920	1020	1220	1420	1620
HEATHROW AIRPORT Terminals 1, 2, 3, & Central Bus station	LHR123O	0420	0550	0725	0830	0955	1050	1155	1355	1555	1755
HEATHROW AIRPORT Departures Terminal 4	LHR4	0430	0600	0745	0850	1015	1110	1215	1415	1615	1815

FLIGHTLINK IS A NO-SMOKING SERVICE   24Hour Free Parking   See Page 6.

1995/1996 edition of the Flightlink timetable. Connecting services were now available from Manchester to Heathrow and Gatwick Airports.

Flights – People to Places in Style

Although the Bova Futuras operated most of the Flightlink departures, three double-deck Neoplan Skyliners were also acquired in 1995. M1 FTG, M2 FTG and M3 FTG are pictured at Long Acre. *Ken Flight collection*

A nearside view of M2 FTG – built to Flight's own specification, these impressive coaches were used on the busiest Heathrow and Gatwick departures and, as with all of the fleet, were also available for private charter. *Ken Flight collection*

A Pictorial History of Flights Coaches

M1 FTG was exhibited in the trade display at the 1995 UK Coach Rally by S J Carlton – importer of Neoplan coaches at the time. Note the two access doors to the luggage hold either side of the rear axles. *Andrew Roberts*

A rear view of M1 FTG. Flight's specification included a reduced seating capacity of 69 passengers, kitchen area and the staircase re-positioned to face forward. *Andrew Roberts*

Flights – People to Places in Style

1996 – Six Plaxton Excalibur bodied Volvo coaches were purchased this year. The first three had B10M chassis with 49-seats – including 2 FTG pictured on Madeira Drive, Brighton at the UK Coach Rally. *Andrew Roberts*

FTG 5 was another of the Volvo B10M – Plaxton Excaliburs and is pictured at Aston Hall in Birmingham. These coaches, and all future new vehicles, were painted in a revised version of the fleet livery – to match the Flightlink Bovas of 1994 and 96. *Andrew Roberts collection*

The three other Plaxton bodied coaches acquired in 1996 were of the Volvo B10MSE type and were the first Excaliburs built on this chassis. N9 FTG was fitted with 36-seats and tables for corporate hires. *Daniel Hill photography*

The B10MSE chassis offered enhanced luggage space as the engine was positioned further towards the rear of the vehicle. The chassis was supplied to Plaxton as a short underframe with the centre section built by the bodybuilder. The extended wheelbase is evident in this view of N8 FTG. *PM photography*

Flights – People to Places in Style

Flights secured the contract to operate car park shuttle buses at the National Exhibition Centre in 1996. A fleet of ten Dennis Darts with Plaxton Pointer bodies were acquired – P10 FTG and P9 FTG are pictured at Long Acre when new. *Pete Southern*

The new contract specified low floor easy access buses – the service had previously been operated with high floor coaches. A dedicated livery in white with blue and red "NEC" logo was originally applied to these vehicles – as demonstrated by P4 FTG pictured here in service. *Daniel Hill photography*

A further new coach delivered in September 1996 was the V.I.P. Executive specification Scania K113TRB with Irizar Century bodywork. Allocated cherished registration, 1 FTO, this coach was designated as the new team coach for Aston Villa. *Tony Greaves / Ken Flight collection*

This coach was painted in a special silver based livery with "Hospitality on the move" lettering. The interior included 32 leather seats, tables, kitchen, satellite TV, extra dark tinted windows etc. *Tony Greaves / Ken Flight collection*

Flights – People to Places in Style

1997 – Two further tri-axle Scanias with Irizar Century bodies entered the fleet this year. Painted in Flight's cream and black livery, these coaches were built to touring specification with 51-seats and were allocated "cherished" registrations, F11 GHT ("Flight") and L1 NER ("Liner"). F11 GHT is pictured at Scania UK prior to delivery. *Andrew Roberts collection*

1 FTO and F11 GHT were entered in the 1997 UK Coach Rally – the pair are seen here on Madeira Drive, Brighton. *Andrew Roberts*

A nearside view of F11 GHT – this coach was judged "Top Touring Coach". Note that the black and silver stripes are staggered along the side of the coach. *Andrew Roberts*

1 FTO was awarded the "Coach of the Year" title at Brighton, as well as best Scania and best Irizar. Ken Flight, Geoff Flight and crew receive their trophies from former South East Traffic Commissioner Chris Heaps. *Ken Flight collection*

Flights – People to Places in Style

Coach Charter brochure – late 1990's. The strap line "People to Places in Style" was displayed on the sides of the Private Hire fleet and all associated publicity.

138

A Pictorial History of Flights Coaches

FTG 567, a 10-metre Bova Futura – acquired new in August 1997. This was the first example of the short model Bova to be supplied to a UK operator. *Andrew Roberts*

A rear view of FTG 567 – this coach was fitted with 34-seats and had all of the features of larger coaches in the fleet, including a toilet /washroom and kitchen servery thus making an ideal touring coach for smaller groups. *Ken Flight collection*

Flights – People to Places in Style

The coaching division of West Midlands Travel, Central Coachways, was taken over in November 1997. Seventeen vehicles, including Bova Futuras, Van-Hool bodied DAFs and Ikarus bodied Volvos, were acquired but disposed of early in 1998. Six of the acquired coaches are pictured here at Flights Long Acre depot. *Ken Flight collection*

A PCV driver training school was set-up in 1997 and this former Ministry of Defence Dodge with a Wadham Stringer body was acquired. Originally registered 93 KF 29, it was re-registered E330 WOK for its civilian career. *Ken Flight collection*

A Pictorial History of Flights Coaches

Two more Caetano Optimo mini coaches were purchased in 1997 including P77 FTG, which is pictured at Warwick Castle whilst transporting guests of Jaguar – one of Flight's corporate clients. *Andrew Roberts*

A publicity photograph – circa 1997, with Toyota-Caetano Optimo, Plaxton Premiere bodied Dennis Javelin and Irizar Century – Scania posed for the camera at Kenilworth Castle in Warwickshire. *Ken Flight collection*

Flights – People to Places in Style

Group Travel brochure produced late 1990's with sample packages of UK and European tours for group organisers.

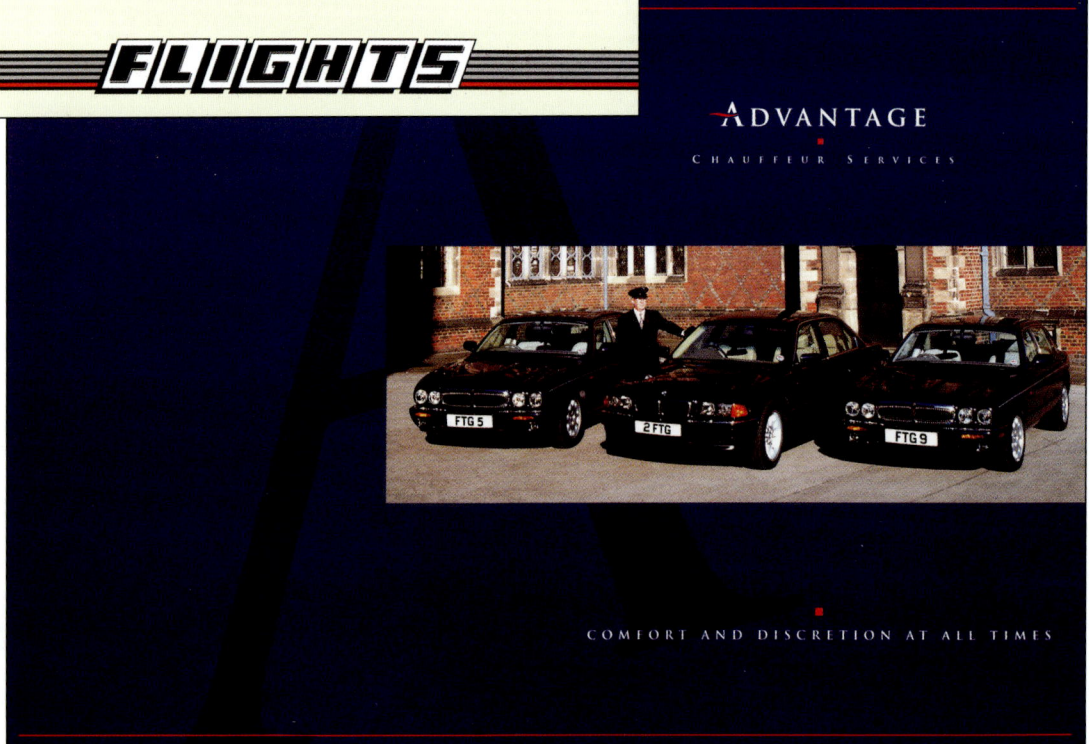

An expanding corporate client list kept the coach fleet busy throughout the year. A new division, "Advantage Chauffeur Services", also offered these clients chauffeur driven cars and people carriers.

142

A Pictorial History of Flights Coaches

Five Plaxton Premiere 320 bodied Dennis Javelins entered service in November 1997 – all were 53-seaters and formed part of the private hire fleet. One of the batch; R773 WOB is pictured at Cadbury World, Birmingham. *Andrew Roberts*

A nearside view of R774 WOB – these coaches served in the fleet until 2001, and although no further examples were purchased, Ken Flight recalls that they gave excellent service. *Andrew Roberts*

Flights – People to Places in Style

1998 – Six more Plaxton Excalibur bodied Volvos were acquired this year – all received A – FTG registrations from new. A3 FTG, a 49-seat B10M is pictured whilst on tour in Austria for tour operator Travelsphere. *Ken Flight collection*

A5 FTG was another B10M from the batch – Flight's smart livery suited these vehicles well – the additional marker and roof lights add the finishing touch. *Andrew Roberts*

144

A Pictorial History of Flights Coaches

A8 FTG was another of the 1998 Plaxton bodied Volvos but was a B10MSE model. The coach is pictured at the UK Coach Rally with driver Mick Howell competing in the "Coach Driver of the Year" final test – Mick was runner-up in the competition. *Ken Flight collection*

A rear view of A8 FTG – note that this coach does not have a rear window fitted allowing a greater area for sign writing. This was a feature on some, but not all, vehicles in the fleet. *Ken Flight collection*

Flights – People to Places in Style

Harrington Cavalier bodied AEC Reliance, 477 AOP, new in 1960 to Flight's Tours was re-acquired by the company in the late 1980's after being discovered in a semi-derelict condition. The coach was stripped and refurbished to bring it back to concours condition. *Ken Flight collection*

477 AOP at Long Acre prior to restoration – after service with Flights it was sold to Hall's Coaches, Rock End and then stored by them after being withdrawn from service. *Ken Flight collection*

The interior was completely re-built, and a set of Chapman reclining seats installed after being re-upholstered in original pattern mocquette. *Ken Flight collection*

After a re-paint into cream and black, traditional sign writing (not vinyl!) was applied to the boot doors. *Ken Flight collection*

A Pictorial History of Flights Coaches

When completed, 477 AOP returned to Brighton in April 1998 to take part in the UK Coach Rally – an event that the coach was entered, when new, some 34 years earlier. In this view the coach is seen at the 1999 event where it was awarded the Michelin Gold Award in the concours competition. *Andrew Roberts*

An interior view of 477 AOP after restoration – the Chapman reclining seats and tables were as fitted when new. Although no longer owned by the Flight family, the coach can often be seen at transport events around the country. *Ken Flight collection*

Flights – People to Places in Style

Following the sale of Flightlink to National Express, Flights continued to operate services on contract. Six new Volvo B10MSE chassis with Plaxton Premiere 350 bodies were acquired for these duties in 1998, including S365 OOB pictured here. *Daniel Hill photography*

Another of the batch, S295 WOA, is pictured at Digbeth Coach Station, Birmingham. National Express adopted a simplified version of the Flight's Flightlink livery, which was applied to all vehicles serving UK airports. *Ken Flight collection*

A Pictorial History of Flights Coaches

2000 – Six of Plaxton's new Panther body with Volvo B10M chassis were acquired this year – registered W2-W7 FTG. One of the six is pictured here in Plaxton's hometown of Scarborough prior to delivery. *Plaxton*

Plaxton Panther bodied Volvo B10M, W7 FTG, pictured in Stratford upon Avon. *Andrew Roberts*

Flights – People to Places in Style

This high specification Neoplan Starliner N516 SHD joined the fleet in October 2000. Allocated the flagship registration of 1 FTO, this 32-seat super executive became the latest coach to transport the Aston Villa FC team to away matches. Pictured here in April 2001 on Madeira Drive, Brighton, the coach was one of three Flights entrants in the UK Coach Rally. *Stuart Jones*

A Pictorial History of Flights Coaches

The high specification of this coach included 32 leather seats, tables, galley kitchen and a full entertainment system. For corporate and special hires catering and hostess service was available. *Ken Flight collection*

Flights earned their 6th "Coach of the Year" award with this coach – it also won the best Neoplan trophy and the Telma trophy. Left to right: Geoff Flight, Dave Wood, Paul Williams, Ken Flight and Chris Heaps at the awards ceremony. *Stuart Jones*

Flights – People to Places in Style

Flights were amongst the first customers for the new Volvo B12M chassis when it was introduced to the UK. Two were acquired in 2001 including A3 FTG, which was the second of Flight's entries at this years UK Coach Rally. *Andrew Roberts*

A rear view of A3 FTG – the sticker in the rear window is confirmation of Flight's membership of "Coach Marque" – a quality assurance scheme backed by the Confederation of Passenger Transport. *Ken Flight collection*

A Pictorial History of Flights Coaches

More awards for Flights at the 2001 UK Coach Rally – Driver Mick Howell (centre) and co-driver, receive the Plaxton and Volvo trophies from Chris Heaps. *Stuart Jones*

Flight's second Plaxton Panther bodied B12M, A4 FTG, was exhibited by Volvo in the trade display at the rally. *Andrew Roberts*

153

Flights – People to Places in Style

The restoration was completed in time to take TOB 377 to the 2001 UK Coach Rally at Brighton – where it is pictured here on Madeira Drive looking as good as the day that it left the Burlingham factory – 46 years earlier. *Andrew Roberts*

An offside view of restored TOB 377. Ken Flight kept a record of every part of the restoration – although no account is available for the cost. The coach was kept by the Flight family at the Aston Manor Transport Museum in Birmingham until being sold in 2010. *Andrew Roberts*

A Pictorial History of Flights Coaches

A view of the completed interior after refurbishment. *Ken Flight collection*

The restored cab area. *Ken Flight collection*

Interior view looking forward. *Ken Flight collection*

Flights – People to Places in Style

TOB 377, arriving at Long Acre after being stored for a number of years at the Transport Museum in Wythall. *Ken Flight collection*

All of the mouldings on the exterior were removed and the bodywork repaired and prepared for re-painting. *Ken Flight collection*

The interior was completely stripped and re-built. *Ken Flight collection*

Flights Coach Travel – Fleet list

Reg.	Chassis	Body	Seats	New	Bought	Sold	Note
OB 4812	Austin 2/3 ton		Ch14	1914	?	?	Ex Army
OE 6233	Daimler		CH24	1920	?	?	
AJ 8353	Daimler 22hp		Ch28	1922	4/24	12/28	Ex Robinson, Scarborough
OP 7000	Chevrolet LM		C14	1927	4/27	?	
VP 7700	Daimler CRA		CH26	1929	3/29	?	
VP 7882	Daimler CF6	Rees & Griffiths	C32	1929	4/29	?	
EK 7574	Daimler CF6		C26	1930	5/34	?	Ex Hickson, Tamworth
OJ 1156	Maudslay ML3E	Rushton & Wilson	C32	1932	7/34	5/49	Ex Hopkins, Birmingham
DOE 227	Bedford WTB	Auto Cellulose	C26F	1937	5/37	5/53	
JW 7224	Maudslay SF40	Burlingham	C35F	1935	6/46	12/52	Ex Turner Crowland
HOL 250	Maudslay Marathon	Santus	C33F	1948	1/48	4/56	
JOM 797	Austin CXB	Mann Egerton	C31F	1949	5/49	4/54	
JVP 700	Maudslay Marathon	Windover	C33F	1949	8/49		
LOX 700	AEC Regal IV	Burlingham Seagull	C37C	1951	12/51	4/60	
KDG 523	" "	" "	C37C	1951	5/53	7/59	Ex Norton, Lechlade
OON 707	" "	" "	C37C	1954	4/54	11/63	
NOF 550	" "	" "	C37C	1953	11/55	10/63	Ex LF Bowen, Birmingham
TOB 377	AEC Reliance	Burlingham Seagull	C37C	1956	3/56	2/65	
477 AOP	AEC Reliance	Harrington Cavalier	C25F	1960	3/60	2/66	
577 DOG	" "	" "	C41F	1961	2/61	2/66	
677 DOF	" "	" "	C25F	1961	4/61	2/66	
ROE 10	Bedford SBG	Duple Vega	C38F	1955	4/61	2/62	Ex Grimsley, Birmingham
ROE 11	" "	" "	C38F	1955	4/61	2/62	" " "
TOF 3	" "	" "	C41F	1956	4/61	3/63	" " "
32 BCG	Ford Thames 570E	Duple Yeoman	C41F	19??	2/62	1/66	Ex Banstead Coaches
877 FOH	" "	" "	C41F	1962	2/62	1/66	
777 FOH	AEC Reliance	Plaxton Panorama	C39F	1962	4/62	4/66	
977 JOB	" "	" "	C37F	1963	4/63		8/65 Burnt out
717 MOB	" "	" "	C37F	1964	4/64		Became YOB 710J
727 MOB	Ford Thames 676E	Plaxton Panorama	C45F	1964	4/64	11/68	
737 MOB	" "	" "	C51F	1964	4/64	7/67	
747 MOH	" "	" "	C51F	1964	4/64	3/68	
707 MOP	" "	" "	C51F	1964	5/64	11/68	
739 MTF	Ford Thames 570E	Burlingham Seagull 60	C41F	1960	5/64	1/65	Ex Sugden, Birmingham
757 MOP	AEC Reliance	Plaxton Panorama	C51F	1964	7/64		9/64 Burnt out
COL 787C	Ford Thames 676E	Plaxton Panorama I	C52F	1965	4/65	11/69	
COL 797C	" "	" " "	C52F	1965	4/65	2/70	
COL 767C	" "	" " "	C52F	1965	5/65	2/70	
COM 777C	" "	" " "	C52F	1965	5/65	11/69	
BNW 627C	AEC Reliance	Plaxton Panorama I	C51F	1965	2/66	7/74	Ex Wallace Arnold
BNW 628C	" "	" " "	C51F	1965	2/66	4/72	" " "
CUM 533C	" "	" " "	C43F	1965	2/66	2/71	" " "
FOP 701D	" "	" " "	C45F	1966	4/66	11/73	
FOP 702D	" "	" " "	C37F	1966	4/66	11/73	
JON 700E	Bristol RELH6L	Plaxton Panorama I	C49F	1967	4/67	12/71	
KOE 703E	Ford R192	Plaxton Panorama I	C45F	1967	5/67	5/71	
ROE 704G	AEC Reliance	Plaxton Panorama Elite	C49F	1969	7/69	11/73	
ROE 705G	" "	" " "	C49F	1969	7/69	11/73	
UOM 707H	" "	" " "	C55F	1970	5/70	11/73	
UOM 708H	" "	" " "	C51F	1970	6/70	11/73	
UOM 709H	" "	" " "	C51F	1970	6/70	11/73	
YOB 710J	AEC Reliance	Plaxton Panorama Elite II	C53F	1971	5/71	11/73	717 MOB re-bodied
YOB 720J	" "	" " " "	C57F	1971	6/71	11/73	
YOB 730J	" "	" " " "	C57F	1971	6/71	11/73	
YOB 740J	" "	" " " "	C51F	1971	6/71	11/73	
556 AFJ	AEC Reliance	Harrington Cavalier	C36F	1960	12/71	11/73	Ex Greenslades, Exeter
557 AFJ	" "	" "	C41F	1960	12/71	11/73	" " "
558 AFJ	" "	" "	C41F	1960	12/71	11/73	" " "
559 AFJ	" "	" "	C41F	1960	12/71	11/73	" " "
555 AFJ	" "	" "	C40F	1960	4/71	11/73	" " "
554 AFJ	" "	" "	C40F	1960	6/72	11/73	" " "
CVP 770K	AEC Reliance	Plaxton Panorama Elite II	C57F	1972	4/72	11/73	
CVP 750K	" "	" " " "	C57F	1972	5/72	11/73	

November 1973 – coaching fleet and Berners Street Garage sold to L F Bowen
June 1977 – re-commenced coach operating under Forward Coaches name – then Flights Coach Travel from 1979

Reg.	Chassis	Body	Seats	New	Bought	Sold	Note
ROE 700R	Leyland Leopard PSU3D/4R	Plaxton Viewmaster Express	C53F	1977	6/77	5/84	Originally Forward
ROE 701R	" " "	" " "	C53F	1977	6/77	11/83	" "
ROE 703R	" " "	" " "	C53F	1977	6/77	9/83	" "
SOJ 702S	" " "	" " "	C53F	1977	8/77	5/84	" "
SOJ 704S	" " "	" " "	C48FT	1977	8/77	5/84	" "
COF 705V	Leyland Leopard PSU3E/4R	Plaxton Supreme IV Express	C53F	1979	8/79	4/83	
COF 707V	" " "	" " "	C53F	1979	8/79	4/83	
GOP 708W	Volvo B58-61	Plaxton Viewmaster IV Exp.	C53F	1980	10/80	2/85	
GOP 709W	" "	" " "	C53F	1980	10/80	2/85	
GOP 710W	" "	" " "	C53F	1980	10/80	3/85	
GOP 720W	" "	" " "	C53F	1980	10/80	2/85	
GOP 730W	" "	" " "	C53F	1980	10/80	3/85	
NMJ 298V	AEC Reliance	Duple Dominant II	C53F	1979	6/81	6/82	Non-livery (leased)
NMJ 328V	" "	" "	C53F	1979	11/81	6/82	" " "
NOX 750X	Van-Hool T815	Van-Hool Acron	C49FT	1982	4/82	5/86	
NOX 770X	" "	" "	C49FT	1982	4/82	6/85	
NOX 777X	" "	" "	C49FT	1982	4/82	10/85	
NOX 740X	" "	" "	C49FT	1982	5/82	4/85	
DBH 451X	Leyland Leopard PSU5C/4R	Plaxton Supreme IV	C57F	1982	7/82	7/83	Leased from Arlington
DBH 452X	" "	" "	C57F	1982	7/82	4/83	" " "
DBH 453X	Leyland Leopard PSU5D/5R	Duple Dominant III	C57F	1982	7/82	4/83	" " "
DBH 454X	Leyland Leopard PSU3E/4R	Duple Dominant III	C53F	1982	7/82	4/83	" " "
TOA 707Y	Van-Hool T818	Van-Hool Astron	CH50/10DT	1983	6/83	8/85	
TOA 717Y	" "	" "	"	1983	6/83	4/87	
TOA 727Y	" "	" "	"	1983	6/83	7/86	
TOA 737Y	" "	" "	"	1983	6/83	8/85	
TOA 747Y	" "	" "	"	1983	6/83	8/85	
B700 EOF	Scania K112CRS	Jonckheere Jubilee P599	C51FT	1985	5/85	5/88	
B701 EOF	" "	" " "	C51FT	1985	5/85	5/88	
B702 EOF	" "	" " "	C51FT	1985	5/85	5/88	
B703 EOF	" "	" " "	C51FT	1985	5/85	7/88	
B704 EOF	" "	" " "	C51FT	1985	5/85	5/88	
B705 EOF	Volvo B10MT-53	Jonckheere Jubilee P95	CH54/13DT	1985	6/85	9/89	
B707 EOF	" "	" "	"	1985	6/85	5/88	
B708 EOF	" "	" "	"	1985	6/85	1988	
B709 EOF	" "	" "	"	1985	6/85	6/89	
B710 EOF	" "	" "	"	1985	6/85	6/89	
B711 EOF	" "	" "	"	1985	6/85	6/90	
C712 GOP	" "	" "	"	1985	8/85	7/89	Re-reg 278 CFC 2/88
C720 GOP	Volvo B10MT-53	Plaxton Paramount 4000RS	CH54/13CT	1986	4/86	12/90	
C740 GOP	" "	" "	"	1986	4/86	4/90	
C730 GOP	" "	" "	"	1986	3/86	4/90	
C750 GOP	" "	" "	"	1986	4/86	3/96	
C770 GOP	Kassbohrer Setra	Setra S228DT	CH54/20CT	1986	3/86	1/91	Re-reg 278 CFC 11/87 and 1 FTO 3/88
278 CFC	Volvo B10M-61	Duple Caribbean	C36FT	1983	8/87	12/90	Ex Manor Pond, Horley Re-reg FTG 5 11/87
E177 VJW	Volvo B10M-61	Plaxton Paramount III 3500LS		C49FT	1988	5/88	7/92
E277 VJW	" "	" " "	"		1988	5/88	7/92
E377 VJW	" "	" " "	"		1988	5/88	2/93	Re-reg FTG 567 8/91 Re-seated to C32FT 12/91
E477 VJW	" "	" " "	"		1988	5/88	11/92
E577 VJW	" "	" " "	"		1988	5/88	3/93	Re-reg FTG 9 1991
GHH 256N	Bristol LHS6L	Plaxton Supreme	C35F	1974	5/88	6/90	Re-reg FTG 567 9/88
E677 VJW	Volvo B10MT-53	Plaxton Paramount 4000RS	CH54/13CT	1988	6/88	1/91	
E777 VJW	" "	" "	"	1988	6/88	6/91	
F700 COA	" "	" "	"	1989	4/89	4/95	
F701 COA	" "	" "	"	1989	4/89	5/95	
F702 COA	" "	" "	"	1989	4/89	9/95	
F703 COA	Volvo B10MT-53	Plaxton Paramount 4000RS	CH54/13CT	1989	4/89	9/95	
F704 COA	" "	" "	"	1989	5/89	6/94	
F705 COA	" "	" "	"	1989	5/89	12/92	
F707 COA	" "	" "	"	1989	5/89	12/92	
F708 COA	" "	" "	"	1989	6/89	6/94	
F709 COA	" "	" "	"	1989	5/89	8/95	
F710 COA	" "	" "	"	1989	6/89	12/95	

A Pictorial History of Flights Coaches

Reg.	Chassis	Body	Seats	New	Bought	Sold	Note
G717 JOG	Volvo B10MT-53	Plaxton Paramount 4000RS	CH55/12DT	1990	4/90	3/97	Re-reg FTG 5 8/94 and A3 FTG 2/96
G720 JOG	" "	" "	"	1990	4/90	6/97	Re-reg 2 FTG 8/94 and A2 FTG 2/96
G727 JOG	" "	" "	"	1990	4/90	7/97	Re-reg FTG 9 8/94 and A4 FTG 2/96
D793 SGB	Bedford YMP	Plaxton Paramount III 3200	C35F	1987	1990	11/93	Ex Park Hamilton, re-reg FTG 5 1/91
D602 TMR	" "	" " "	C31F	1987	5/90	3/92	Ex Bell, Winterslow, re-reg FTG 567 5/90 and FTG 9 7/91
H2 FTG	Toyota Coaster	Caetano Optimo II	C18F	1991	5/91	5/98	
H3 FTG	" "	" "	C18F	1991	5/91	9/97	
J451 UFS	Mercedes-Benz 811D	PMT Ami	C35F	1992	2/92	6/95	Re-reg J10 FTG 3/92
J457 UFS	" "	" "	C35F	1992	3/92	7/95	Re-reg J7 FTG 3/92
J8 FTG	" "	" "	C35F	1992	3/92	10/95	
J4 FTG	Toyota Coaster	Caetano Optimo II	C21F	1992	6/92	3/97	
J6 FTG	" "	" "	C21F	1992	6/92	6/97	
K285 XOG	Volvo B10M-60	Plaxton Excalibur	C49FT	1992	8/92	5/96	Re-reg K12 FTG 1/93
K286 XOG	" "	" "	C49FT	1992	8/92	12/97	Re-reg K14 FTG 1/93
K15 FTG	" "	" "	C49FT	1993	1/93	11/95	
K16 FTG	" "	" "	C49FT	1993	1/93	5/96	
K17 FTG	" "	" "	C49FT	1993	1/93	5/96	
K18 FTG	" "	" "	C49FT	1993	2/93	5/96	
K19 FTG	" "	" "	C49FT	1993	3/93	5/97	
K20 FTG	" "	" "	C49FT	1993	3/93	4/98	
1 FTO	Bova	Bova Futura FHD12-290	C25FT	1989	2/93	8/96	Ex Central Coachways F907 CJW / 245 DOC
L11 FTG	Bova	Bova Futura FHD 12-340	C44FT	1994	5/94	5/00	Re-reg L1 NER 8/94
L22 FTG	"	" " "	C44FT	1994	5/94	6/01	
L33 FTG	"	" " "	C44FT	1994	5/94	4/00	
L44 FTG	"	" " "	C44FT	1994	5/94	5/01	
L55 FTG	"	" " "	C44FT	1994	5/94	5/00	
L66 FTG	"	" " "	C44FT	1994	5/94	1999	
L77 FTG	"	" " "	C44FT	1994	5/94	4/00	
L1 NKF	"	" " "	C44FT	1994	5/94	1/00	
M1 FTG	Neoplan N122	Neoplan Skyliner	CH57/12DT	1995	5/95	4/00	
M2 FTG	" "	" "	"	1995	5/95	6/00	
M3 FTG	" "	" "	"	1995	5/95	9/02	
M10 FTG	Bova	Bova Futura FHD 12-340	C44FT	1995	5/95	8/00	
M20 FTG	"	" " "	C44FT	1995	5/95	8/00	
M30 FTG	"	" " "	C44FT	1995	4/95	8/00	
M40 FTG	"	" " "	C44FT	1995	4/95	7/00	
M50 FTG	"	" " "	C44FT	1995	5/95	3/00	
M60 FTG	"	" " "	C44FT	1995	4/95	5/00	
N495 NVP	Nissan Serena		M7	1995	8/95	?	
2 FTG	Volvo B10M-62	Plaxton Excalibur	C49FT	1996	2/96	3/00	Re-reg N387 DRW 7/99
FTG 5	" "	" "	C49FT	1996	2/96	4/00	Re-reg N389 DRW 9/99
FTG 9	" "	" "	C49FT	1996	2/96	2/00	Re-reg N388 DRW 9/99
N7 FTG	Volvo B10MSE-62	Plaxton Excalibur	C44FT	1996	6/96	2002	
N8 FTG	" "	" "	C44FT	1996	6/96	2002	
N9 FTG	" "	" "	C36FT	1996	6/96	2002	
P1 FTG	Dennis Dart SLF	Plaxton Pointer II	B40F	1996	8/96	*	
P2 FTG	" " "	" " "	B40F	1996	8/96	*	
P3 FTG	" " "	" " "	B40F	1996	8/96	*	
P4 FTG	" " "	" " "	B40F	1996	8/96	*	
P5 FTG	" " "	" " "	B40F	1996	8/96	*	
P6 FTG	" " "	" " "	B40F	1996	8/96	*	
P7 FTG	" " "	" " "	B40F	1996	8/96	*	
P8 FTG	" " "	" " "	B40F	1996	8/96	*	
P9 FTG	" " "	" " "	B40F	1996	8/96	*	
P10 FTG	Dennis Dart SLF	Plaxton Pointer II	B40F	1996	8/96	*	
1 FTO	Scania K113TRB	Irizar Century 12.370	C32FT	1996	9/96	6/02	Re-reg A2 FTG
L1 NER	" "	" "	C51FT	1997	4/97	4/02	
F11 GHT	" "	" "	C51FT	1997	4/97	6/02	

159

Reg.	Chassis	Body	Seats	New	Bought	Sold	Note
P70 FTG	Toyota Coaster	Caetano Optimo III	C18F	1997	4/97	*	
P77 FTG	" "	" " "	C18F	1997	4/97	*	
FTG 567	Bova	Bova Futura FHD 10-340	C34FT	1997	8/97	5/02	
R770 WOB	Dennis Javelin	Plaxton Premiere 320	C53F	1997	10/97	3/01	
R771 WOB	" "	" " "	C53F	1997	11/97	1/01	
R772 WOB	" "	" " "	C53F	1997	11/97	1/01	
R773 WOB	" "	" " "	C53F	1997	11/97	1/01	
R774 WOB	" "	" " "	C53F	1997	11/97	1/01	
FYX 817W	Leyland Leopard PSU3E/4R	Duple Dominant IV	C49F	1980	11/97	12/97	Ex Central Coachways
GIL 2942	DAF SB3000	Van-Hool Alizee SH	C51FT	1988	11/97	3/98	Ex Central Coachways Original reg: E355 EVH
TIA 5734			C51FT	1988	11/97	3/98	Ex Central Coachways Original reg: E357 EVH
HDZ 8350	Bova	Bova Futura FHD 12-290	C49FT	1989	11/97	3/99	Ex Central Coachways Original reg: F920 BVP
HDZ 8352	"	" " "	C49FT	1989	11/97	10/98	Ex Central Coachways Original reg: F77 XUY
G543 JOG	"	" " "	C496FT	1990	11/97	3/99	Ex Central Coachways
5010 CD	"	" " "	C49FT	1990	11/97	10/98	Ex Central Coachways Original reg: G544 JOG
WLT 702	DAF SBR3000	Plaxton Paramount 4000	CH55/19CT	1990	11/97	12/97	Ex Central Coachways Original reg: G776 HOV
MIL 4765	" "	" " "	"	1990	3/90	12/97	Ex Central Coachways Original reg: G778 HOV
H407 LVC	Volvo B10M-60	Ikarus Blue Danube 350	C49FT	1991	11/97	1/98	Ex Central Coachways
H408 LVC	" "	" " "	C49FT	1991	11/97	1/98	" " "
H130 MRW	" "	" " "	C51FT	1991	11/97	1/98	" " "
H131 MRW	" "	" " "	C51FT	1991	11/97	1/98	" " "
J844 RAC	" "	" " "	C53F	1991	11/97	1/98	" " "
J845 RAC	" "	" " "	C53F	1991	11/97	1/98	" " "
N53 FWU	DAF SB3000	Van-Hool Alizee HD	C49FT	1996	11/97	1/98	" " "
N54 FWU	" "	" " "	C49FT	1996	11/97	1/98	" " "
R977 VOG	Mercedes-Benz 108	Mercedes-Benz	8	1997	1997	?	
E330 WOK	Dodge GU63	Wadham Stringer	B38F	1988	1/98	11/01	Ex MOD (93 KF 29)
A3 FTG	Volvo B10M-62	Plaxton Excalibur	C49FT	1998	5/98	1/02	
A4 FTG	" "	" "	C49FT	1998	5/98	2/02	
A5 FTG	" "	" "	C49FT	1998	5/98	7/02	
A6 FTG	" "	" "	C49FT	1998	5/98	9/03	
A7 FTG	" "	" "	C49FT	1998	5/98	7/01	
A8 FTG	" "	" "	C49FT	1998	5/98	*	
S363 OOB	Volvo B10MSE	Plaxton Premiere 350	C49FT	1998	12/98	*	
S365 OOB	" "	" "	C49FT	1998	12/98	*	
S295 WOA	" "	" "	C49FT	1998	12/98	*	
S296 WOA	" "	" "	C49FT	1998	12/98	*	
S297 WOA	" "	" "	C49FT	1998	12/98	*	
S298 WOA	" "	" "	C49FT	1998	12/98	*	
V447 EAL	Volvo B10M	Plaxton Premiere 350	C44FT	1999	11/99	*	
V448 EAL	" "	" "	C44FT	1999	11/99	*	
V449 EAL	" "	" "	C44FT	1999	11/99	*	
W2 FTG	Volvo B10M-62	Plaxton Panther	C49FT	2000	6/00	6/02	
W3 FTG	" "	" "	C49FT	2000	8/00	6/02	
W4 FTG	" "	" "	C49FT	2000	8/00	6/02	
W5 FTG	" "	" "	C49FT	2000	9/00	6/02	
W6 FTG	" "	" "	C49FT	2000	8/00	5/02	
W7 FTG	" "	" "	C49FT	2000	8/00	6/02	
1 FTO	Neoplan	Neoplan Starliner N516SHD	C32FT	2000	10/00	*	
A3 FTG	Volvo B12M-62	Plaxton Panther	C49FT	2001	3/01	8/02	
A4 FTG	" "	" "	C49FT	2001	4/01	2002	

* = Vehicle passed to Dunn-Line 2002

ALSO AVAILABLE FROM BREWIN BOOKS

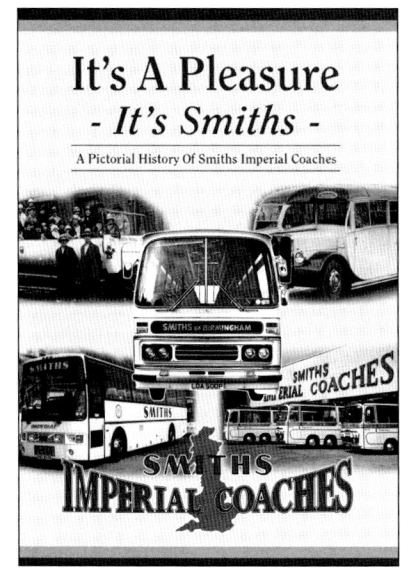

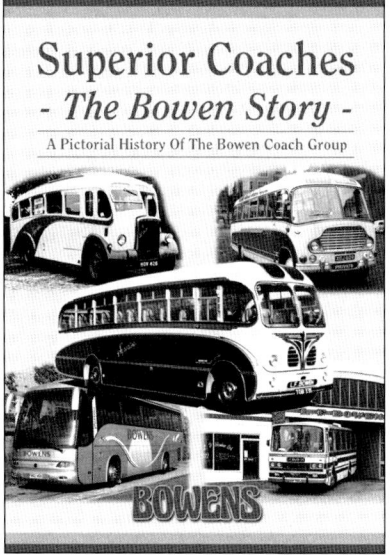

ISBN: 978-1-85858-222-1
PRICE: £10.95

ISBN: 978-1-85858-248-1
PRICE: £14.95

ISBN: 978-1-85858-277-1
PRICE: £10.95